UNLOCK
Your World of Creativity

6 Key Lessons Learned from More Than 250 Creatives Worldwide

UNLOCK
Your World of Creativity

6 Key Lessons Learned from
More Than 250 Creatives
Worldwide

Mark Stinson
Best-selling Author of
N-of-8 and ForwardFast

Foreword by John David Mann

Exact Rush Multimedia Publishing
353 W. Greensboro Ct.
Boise, ID 83706

Exact Rush Multimedia Publishing and the Exact Rush logo
are trademarks of Exact Rush, LLC.

Library of Congress Control Number: 2025922625
ISBN: 979-8-9898235-7-4

To my 5 grandchildren:

May a whole world of creativity be open to you.
May you put your creative fingerprints on it.

CONTENTS

FOREWORD

When I was twelve my mom took a group of school kids to Greece to stage a performance of Prometheus Bound. In preparation for the trip, she decided she'd like to have some of the choruses set to music, so she asked me to do it. Just like that. Like she was asking if I wouldn't mind doing the dishes. "I'm twelve years old!" I protested. "I don't know how to do that! I can't compose concert-quality music out of thin air!"

"Sure, you can," she said.

So, I did. We performed the play in an ancient amphitheater in Epidaurus, and a few years later my compositions won a national award.

That's how creativity happens: when your mom says, hey, we need this, will you do it?

To be fair, I had the advantage of growing up in a family of musicians. Still, I had no such advantage five years later when some friends and I decided to start our own school. We hadn't a clue how to go about doing such a thing, no training or background in entrepreneurship. Hell, we were teenagers. But we were tired of sitting through mediocre classes in our boring schools. We wanted to learn something.

So, we started a high school, and over the next few years, with no certification or accreditation of any kind, we successfully placed our graduates at schools including Harvard, Yale, and state universities across the country.

There's a common myth about creativity, that it arrives like a lightning strike from the heavens above, sparking in the favored few a sort of fever dream of brilliance, a boiling over of inner revelation that cannot be contained.

Nope. That's not how it works. Creativity happens when your mom needs some music for a play and asks you to do it. It happens when you and your friends need a good school and there isn't one around. It happens when, as Mark Stinson tells it in the opening paragraph of this book, some second-graders want to raise money for a worthy cause.

Creativity is not some rarified event unfolding in an ivory tower. Creativity is a natural response to real-world problems, challenges, and opportunities.

Since that fund-raising stint at age 7, Mark has grown up to become one of the most creative people I know. He is an expert witness to the creative process, one who has circled the globe and devoted decades to searching out creatives in every imaginable field of endeavor, reverse-engineering how they work and what they do to achieve their ground-breaking innovations. Some of those enterprises he has collaborated in or masterminded himself. And happily, for you and me, we get to absorb the full weight and wisdom of those decades, distilled here between the two covers of a book.

In this immensely practical user's manual, Mark offers six broad strategies for mastering the process of being a creator—call them distinction, resilience, collaboration, practicality, adaptability, and purpose—each one illustrated with wildly fascinating profiles of real-world creatives of every stripe and discipline.

The first and most important step, however, is one he addresses right off the bat in the introduction and returns to again in his conclusion: decide to be a creator. Make the decision not to be content letting life happen to you; choose instead that you will be something that happens to life.

Creativity starts with intention.

A friend recently asked me, "So, how does the whole writing thing work—do you sit down to write when inspiration strikes?"

"No," I replied, "I sit down to write when the alarm clock goes off."

In these pages you'll learn about composers and authors, marketers and manufacturers, celebrity TV producers, pharmaceutical developers, creators of multinational conglomerates, family businesses, and nonprofits. You'll meet an ethnobotanist-turned-entrepreneur and a C-suite executive who turned to purging plastics from the world's oceans. What this diverse cast of characters all have in common is that they each made the decision to create, then acted with intention. And in doing so, they have changed the world for the better.

What a wonderful word, intention: from the Latin tendere, meaning "to stretch," as in the stretched strings of a loom or musical instrument (where we get our word tendon). To be creative is to stretch yourself. In that stretching is how you grow, how you evolve to become more fully yourself.

The poet Mary Oliver put it this way:

> *The most regretful people on earth are those who felt the call*
> *to creative work, who felt their own creative power restive*
> *and uprising, and gave to it neither power nor time.*

Creativity should be taught in every school, for it is far more essential than spelling or arithmetic. Like leadership, it is available to everyone, everywhere, not something given only to the few, the odd, the particularly talented. And it is not a luxury, a thing we do with the time that's left over from the "important" tasks. Creativity is the engine that drives our very existence. It is how you reinvent yourself, how you maintain your life as something fresh and alive rather than withering away into a resigned husk of itself.

On my dad's seventieth birthday, having arrived at the age of mandatory retirement at his university, he exclaimed, "Ahhh ... now I can really get something done," and for the next two decades he threw himself into writing and publishing project after project. To him, reinvention was more interesting than retirement—and it added two glorious decades to his life.

"Stories are all we have to fight off illness and death," wrote novelist and essayist Leslie Marmon Silko, and you can broaden her word "stories" to embrace all creative acts. Creation is, after all, always a kind of story-telling.

Every culture has its version of the "creation myth." But that fundamental myth finds itself retold every time anyone anywhere says, "Wait a minute, what if we did this, or tried that" . . . and the world is reborn all over again.

So, enjoy and absorb Mark's book—and then go change the world.

— John David Mann, May 2025

INTRODUCTION

I remember the first time someone called me "creative." It was a late-summer afternoon before school started back up. I was in the second grade, and my friends and I had turned our garage into an art gallery for a fundraiser. We'd been working for hours, tacking our colorful creations up on the walls and arranging a few tables to make it look official. Our mission was to raise money for the Muscular Dystrophy Association Telethon that played every Labor Day weekend. I didn't think of myself as an artist back then—I was just excited to see what we could accomplish together.

As we opened our "show" and a few neighbors came by to look, I heard one of them mention to my parents that I was "really creative." I felt proud, of course, but something more clicked that day. Setting up the "gallery" wasn't just about my work; it was about giving my friends a platform for their art, too. I realized that the joy of creating something special could be even better when shared, and that was the moment a seed was planted: creativity wasn't just about making things; it was about amplifying other voices and ideas as well.

That garage art show stayed with me. Later, in school projects and work, I often found myself drawn to collaborating and to finding ways to lift up others' ideas. And years later, it led me to start my podcast, *Your World of Creativity*, where I learn from artists and creators around the world. The second-grade art show in my garage may have been my first "gallery," but in many ways, it's the one that set me on the path I'm on today—discovering, celebrating, and sharing creativity wherever I find it.

What's in Your Hands

Creativity is a powerful force, and in my quest to understand it, I traveled to 50 countries and interviewed 250 creatives. These conversations gave me deep insights into how people from different backgrounds tap into their creativity. This book distills those lessons into strategies that can help anyone unlock their creative potential.

I spoke with professionals from all kinds of fields—authors, actors, marketers, musicians, chefs, hotel managers, a toy inventor, and even a game show creator. I also had a surprising conversation with a celebrity dentist, which showed me that creativity truly has no boundaries. The diversity of these voices shaped my understanding of creativity and reinforced how universal it is.

Through these interviews, I noticed common themes. No matter the discipline or country, every creative shared a passion for their work, an innovative mindset, and a drive to express themselves. These shared experiences helped me identify key strategies that can guide anyone looking to harness their own creativity.

Strategic Crafting: Building Your Unique Creative Position

The question that came up again and again during my interviews was: How does someone get unstuck in their creative process?

It's a challenge that every creative person faces at some point—whether you're staring at a blank page or feeling stuck in a project. What I found is that the key to moving forward lies in developing a clear, actionable strategy. A strategy not only helps you break through creative blocks, but it also opens up new possibilities for your work.

One of the first steps in this process is defining your unique creative position and honing your voice. It's not just about producing more work—it's about creating with purpose and intention. For example, one author I spoke with struggled for years to complete a novel. It wasn't until she focused on writing from her specific life experiences and stopped trying to fit into a genre mold that she found her creative flow. Once she defined her voice, the writing process became more natural, and she completed her novel in just a few months.

Creating with purpose means understanding why you're making something and what impact you want it to have. Intention is about being deliberate in your choices—whether it's the materials you use, the stories you tell, or the audience you're speaking to. In today's crowded creative world, standing out requires more than just producing good work. You need a clear vision of what sets you apart. For instance, many musicians today face the challenge of being heard in an oversaturated industry. Those who succeed often do so by identifying a unique angle or style that resonates deeply with their audience.

By applying the lessons from creatives around the world, you can develop a strategy that helps you tap into your full potential and create work that not only breaks through creative blocks but truly stands out.

The 6 Lessons for Success in Creativity

At the core of this book are six proven strategies, drawn from the advice and experiences of the creatives I met across the globe. Each chapter explores one of these strategies, backed by real-world examples, expert stories, and practical steps. These strategies aren't just theories—they are actionable lessons that you can apply to your creative work.

1. Identifying Your Signature Methods

The first step in unlocking your creativity is to uncover and nurture your own signature method. Your uniqueness is your strength. For example, a photographer I interviewed developed a style based on blending urban landscapes with traditional portraiture, something she hadn't seen anyone else do. This approach became her hallmark, setting her apart in a crowded field. This chapter will guide you in embracing your distinct perspective and turning it into a creative advantage.

2. Building a Backbone of Resilience

Creative journeys are rarely smooth. Learning to view setbacks as opportunities is essential for growth. I spoke with a musician who faced constant rejection early in his career, but instead of giving up, he used each "no" as motivation to refine his craft. His persistence eventually led to a breakthrough. Resilience is more than a skill—it's a mindset, and this chapter shows how you can develop it to turn challenges into stepping stones.

3. Partnering with Collaborators

Creativity flourishes when we collaborate with others. Working with people from diverse backgrounds opens new perspectives and ideas. A filmmaker I interviewed credited his most successful projects to working with a team of writers and designers who brought different insights to the table. Collaboration not only enhances your creativity, but it can also take your ideas in directions you never imagined. This chapter explores how to build strong creative partnerships.

4. Mastering the Numbers of Your Business

Creativity and business go hand in hand. Many successful creatives understand the importance of managing the financial and strategic sides of their careers. A ceramic artist, for instance, built a thriving business by learning how to price her work correctly, manage her finances, and market herself effectively. Mastering the business side is key to sustaining long-term success, and this chapter provides the tools you need to do it.

5. Anticipating Obstacles in Your Creative Process

The creative process is unpredictable, and the only constant is change. Whether it's a sudden project cancellation or a shift in your industry, being prepared for the unexpected is crucial. One chef I spoke with had to completely reinvent his restaurant during a downturn in tourism. His ability to adapt on the fly saved his business. In this chapter, you'll learn how to anticipate obstacles, create contingency plans, and navigate the twists and turns of your creative path.

6. Developing Your Leadership Influence as a Creative Force

Creativity with purpose creates lasting impact. Whether you're leading a team or working on a personal project, having a clear sense of purpose drives meaningful work. A nonprofit founder I interviewed talked about how his mission to improve access to education fueled every decision he made, from choosing projects to building partnerships. Leading with purpose gives your work depth and direction. This chapter helps you connect your creativity to a larger goal, driving both personal fulfillment and positive change.

How to Navigate Each Lesson: A Personal and Practical Guide

In each lesson, I present a core lesson, weaving it together with stories from the experts I interviewed and drawing from my own experiences. These lessons aren't just abstract ideas—they are real-world insights from the trenches of creativity, where ideas are formed, tested, and polished. Each lesson is designed to be both a reflection on creative principles and a practical guide that helps you apply these strategies to your own work.

At the end of each lesson, you'll find self-evaluation and reflection questions. These aren't just prompts—they're tools to help you dig into your creative process, examine your approach, and identify areas for growth. The aim is to connect the lessons you've learned with real, actionable steps that push your creativity forward. This isn't just theory; it's a bridge between learning and doing.

Creativity has no limits, and the strategies in this book will help you push your creative work and marketing beyond what you thought possible. It's not just about unlocking your potential; it's about unleashing a force that breaks through boundaries and leads you to a world of endless possibilities.

As you begin this journey, I encourage you to dive deep into the stories, lessons, and strategies ahead. Whether you're an experienced creative, an emerging artist, or someone who simply wants to bring more creativity into your life, these strategies are designed to guide you toward a life of limitless expression.

Welcome to the world of creativity *unlocked*.

LESSON ONE

Identifying Your Signature Methods

Creativity is often seen as something fleeting, but in reality, it's a craft that thrives on discipline and a clear process. In my 250 interviews with creatives around the world, one common thread stood out—successful individuals had a unique, recognizable creative process. This chapter explores the importance of developing your own signature method and how it can transform your creative work.

While spontaneity and inspiration are essential, success comes from combining those moments of brilliance with hard work and dedication. The most successful creatives don't wait for inspiration to strike—they build a process that allows them to consistently produce great work. This is especially important for anyone working in a creative field like podcasting, where creating a signature method can become the foundation of your brand and guide you with purpose.

Throughout this chapter, I'll share examples of creatives who have developed their own unique methods. People like Adam Alter, Christof Zürn, and Robin Landa each follow distinct creative processes. Their stories show how a signature method can fuel creativity and set you apart in your field.

What I've learned is that having your own creative process is key to thriving in a crowded landscape. Here's an approach to building a style that both defines your creative identity and serves as an asset in your professional life:

- **Define Your Style**
  Pinpoint the elements that make your work unique—whether it's your preferred media, distinctive themes, or special techniques. Clarity here shapes the essence of your creative identity.

- **Name Your Process**
  Give your approach a memorable name. Labeling your framework or method makes it easier for others to discuss, adopt, and recognize your style.

- **Document Your Method**
  Outline the steps you follow—from idea generation to execution. Creating a structured guide helps you refine your process over time and turn it into a repeatable system.

- **Teach Your Approach**
  Share what you've learned through workshops, tutorials, mentoring, or social media. Helping others apply your method builds authority and fosters a community around your work.

- **Emphasize Your Uniqueness**
  Highlight the points that differentiate your method from others. Show the fresh perspective or innovative slant you bring to your field.

- **Monetize Your Difference**
  Understand the market value of your unique method. Attract clients, sponsors, and partners who appreciate the distinctive advantages you offer.

Following these steps isn't about limiting creativity—it's about creating a supportive framework that frees you to innovate more effectively. This structured approach can open doors for professional growth, collaboration, and financial success.

Now, let's hear from leading creatives whose signature methods have helped them stand out and build lasting careers.

Adam Alter:
The Anatomy of a Breakthrough

Adam Alter, a professor of marketing and psychology at NYU's Stern School of Business, has developed a unique approach to creative problem-solving. His process is laid out in his book, *The Anatomy of a Breakthrough*, which tackles the universal challenge of feeling stuck and provides a guide for moving past creative blocks. In his work, Adam addresses the emotional, cognitive, and actionable aspects of getting unstuck.

One of the central strategies Adam advocates for is recombination—the practice of merging existing ideas, concepts, or elements to create something entirely new. Recombination thrives on bringing together seemingly unrelated components to form innovative outcomes. Whether it's in the arts, sciences, or business, this approach helps break away from conventional thinking. For example, Pixar's storytelling formula, which Adam references, often combines familiar narrative structures with new twists, creating stories that feel both fresh and relatable.

Adam's teaching style reflects his belief in the power of diverse inspiration. He engages students with impactful business examples and emphasizes the value of crowdsourcing and embracing a variety of perspectives. This approach earned him recognition as NYU's Professor of the Year, showing the effectiveness of applying recombination in real-world settings. His method encourages students—and creatives in general—to look beyond perfectionism and focus on action.

In our podcast conversation, Adam highlighted how recombination has been instrumental for many of the world's greatest creatives. He shared stories of famous writers who overcame creative blocks by mixing elements from different genres or periods, as well as examples of business leaders who rethought their strategies by drawing from outside industries. The key takeaway is that creativity isn't about waiting for the perfect idea to strike—it's about pulling together the ideas already around you and forming something new.

For any creative person feeling stuck, Adam's approach offers a practical solution: shift your focus, draw from diverse sources, and act decisively. His insights are invaluable for anyone looking to break through barriers in their creative process.

Christof Zürn: Music Thinking

Christof Zürn is the pioneer behind *Music Thinking*, a unique framework that uses music not just as a source of inspiration but as a tool for organizing creative thought. With a background in digital production, user-centered design, and musicology philosophy, Christof observed how often musical terms were used in collaborative work environments. Terms like harmony, improvisation, syncopation, and crescendo capture the essence of teamwork, adaptability, and the flow of ideas within a group.

He identified these musical terms as powerful metaphors for collaboration:

- Harmony reflects the seamless integration of diverse talents, creating a balanced and productive team environment.

- Syncopation highlights the introduction of unexpected elements or ideas to enhance creativity, similar to off-beat rhythms in music.

- Improvisation emphasizes the need for teams to think on their feet, adapting to challenges and seizing new opportunities, just like musicians in a live performance.

- Conductor likens a project leader or manager to a conductor, coordinating individual efforts toward a unified goal.

- Crescendo signifies the building intensity or momentum during critical phases of a project, such as a looming deadline.

- Riffing refers to the quick, dynamic exchange of ideas between team members, mirroring how musicians exchange musical phrases.

- Solo recognizes moments when individual team members showcase their expertise, similar to a solo performance in music.

- Tempo dictates the pace at which tasks and projects are completed, ensuring consistency and efficiency.

- Score serves as the project roadmap, guiding the team's efforts much like a musical score guides musicians through a composition.

- Pitch relates to the clarity and persuasiveness of ideas presented, akin to the pitch of sound in music.

Applying these metaphors to collaborative work environments fosters a shared understanding and enhances communication, inspiring creativity and innovation within teams.

To bring this approach to life, Christof developed the Music Thinking Stages: Listen, Tune, Play, and Perform. Inspired by the dynamics of jazz, this framework promotes a fluid, natural progression in the creative process. The first stage, Listen, emphasizes the importance of awareness and recognizing patterns in the environment. Tune is about adjusting and refining ideas based on feedback, much like tuning musical instruments. Play involves experimenting and exploring ideas, while Perform represents the final execution, where everything comes together in a polished result.

One of Christof's key tools for encouraging creativity in teams is the use of Jam Cards in his workshops. These visually appealing cards provide prompts designed to trigger creative responses and inspire innovative thinking, whether in group settings or individual projects. They offer a structured yet flexible way to foster brainstorming and collaboration, making sessions dynamic and enjoyable.

Beyond his work in corporate creativity, Christof is passionate about addressing global challenges. Through his involvement with The Medinge Group and its initiative Generation Co, Christof promotes a planet-first approach, uniting individuals around shared values for positive collective impact. His philosophy challenges traditional generational divides, focusing instead on collaboration for the greater good. *Music Thinking* is not just about fostering creativity in business but also about driving purpose-driven solutions to global problems.

Christof's *Music Thinking* approach revolutionizes how we approach creativity, blending structure with flexibility in much the same way jazz musicians improvise within a framework. His emphasis on inclusivity and collaboration creates a dynamic and purpose-driven environment where creativity can thrive, whether it's in business, personal projects, or tackling global challenges.

Robin Landa: 'The New Art of Ideas'

Robin Landa, an ideation expert and author of *The New Art of Ideas: Unlock Your Creative Potential*, offers a fresh and practical approach to creative idea generation. In her book, Robin introduces the 3G approach—Goal, Gap, Gain—which serves as a flexible framework for developing creative ideas. The beauty of this method lies in its fluidity; you can start with any of the three components depending on the situation. This flexibility challenges the common belief that creativity is something innate that can't be taught, a misconception Robin confronts with her extensive experience teaching creative professionals in fields like advertising, branding, and design.

Her 3G approach breaks down as follows:

- Goal: Identify what you aim to achieve with your creative idea. What is the purpose or problem you're trying to solve?

- Gap: Pinpoint what's missing. What void exists in the current landscape that your idea can fill?

- Gain: Determine the benefit. What value or improvement does your idea bring to the table?

Robin's method not only makes creativity accessible but also highlights the importance of curiosity, good listening, and openness to diverse perspectives. Her approach demystifies the creative process by showing that it can be cultivated and refined. For instance, Robin shares the story of Sal Khan and the creation of

Khan Academy. Khan's curiosity and ability to identify a gap in the education system led to an innovative, widely-used solution.

Collaboration plays a crucial role in Robin's creative philosophy. In *The New Art of Ideas*, she points to her own collaborations, such as working with illustrator Holly Taylor and Broadway director Lauren Laro, as examples of how teamwork can elevate creative projects. These partnerships not only showcase the importance of diversity in thought but also reinforce the idea that creativity flourishes when multiple perspectives are brought together.

Overcoming emotional obstacles is another key theme in Robin's work. She addresses internal and external challenges that creatives often face—such as self-doubt, time management, and the fear of failure. Robin emphasizes the importance of analyzing goals and managing emotional hurdles, encouraging readers to confront these obstacles head-on. Her practical advice is further supported by resources like worksheets and fill-in-the-blank notes, which foster a more interactive, read-and-respond experience. This allows readers to actively engage with the material and apply it to their own creative journeys.

By blending structured methods with practical tools, Robin's *The New Art of Ideas* is a valuable resource for creatives looking to unlock their potential. Her focus on collaboration, curiosity, and emotional resilience offers a comprehensive guide for anyone seeking to generate meaningful, innovative ideas.

Robin is optimistic about the next generation's passion for social justice, environmental concerns, and holding true to their values. She he finds inspiration in her students' commitment to positive change. My conversation with Robin revealed real-world insights into unleashing creativity and overcoming barriers.

Olesija Saue: 'A Brand Named You'

Olesija Saue, a personal branding and executive development expert from Estonia, provided insightful guidance during her interview on the *Unlocking Your World of Creativity* podcast. Her expertise centers on the importance of personal branding in today's connected world, with a strong focus on authenticity, passion, and strategic self-presentation. In her book, *A Brand Named You*, Olesija offers a practical guide with a hundred steps to help individuals understand, strategize, and execute their personal branding efforts effectively.

According to Olesija, personal branding isn't just about self-promotion—it's about managing how others perceive you, both in person and online. In the digital age, individuals have two personal brands: their physical and digital presence. Understanding and managing both is essential for creating opportunities and maintaining consistency across all platforms. Olesija highlights the importance of strategically showcasing your strengths, values, and personal story to attract your ideal target audience.

One of the key challenges in personal branding is overcoming the perception that it's self-indulgent or vain. Olesija tackled this misconception by explaining that everyone already has a personal brand, whether they actively manage it or not. With the rise of social media, the ability to shape and manage your personal brand is more important than ever, as it can open doors and create opportunities. Rather than seeing it as vanity, Olesija frames personal branding as a tool for controlling the narrative of who you are and what you stand for.

Authenticity is a central theme in Olesija's philosophy. She emphasizes the importance of being genuine both online and offline, accepting your strengths and weaknesses, and presenting yourself truthfully. As she puts it, "Your personal brand is what people say about you when you've left the room," echoing Jeff Bezos' famous quote. This lasting impression makes authenticity the cornerstone of a strong personal brand.

During the podcast, the conversation also ventured into the corporate world, where Olesija shared her experience in helping bring the Forbes brand to Estonia. She discussed the unique challenges of introducing a globally recognized brand to a local market, underscoring the need to align the brand with local values and highlight regional success stories. This example illustrated the broader concept that while branding can have universal elements, it must also resonate with local audiences to be effective.

Olesija also stressed the role of curiosity in nurturing creativity and innovation. Drawing inspiration from Estonia's rich history and natural beauty, she spoke about the importance of maintaining a sense of wonder—especially in education—to foster the next generation of innovators. Childhood curiosity, she argued, should be encouraged to promote a lifelong love of learning and creative thinking.

Looking ahead, Olesija predicts an even deeper integration of digital and physical spaces in personal branding. She anticipates a hybrid model, where online interactions lead to meaningful offline connections. In this increasingly connected world, personal brands will serve as trust anchors, helping individuals build authentic relationships across both realms. Despite the growing digital landscape, Olesija remains confident that authenticity and genuine relationships will continue to be key drivers of success.

N-of-8 Groups: My Signature Method

I have worked over the years to develop my own signature toolbox of methodologies. One model is N-of-8 Groups — a facilitation model that brings together a diverse group of eight individuals to generate ideas, evaluate them, and create actionable plans. This method not only encourages collaboration but also ensures that the ideas lead to measurable outcomes, from innovative products and services to marketing differentiation and financial results. N-of-8 helps creatives build processes that go beyond brainstorming, fostering real innovation with a clear pathway to execution.

Here's how I summarize the technique:

What is N-of-8?

- A creative facilitation model built around a group of eight diverse individuals.

Who does N-of-8?

- A trained group moderator leads an innovation team through the process.

When is N-of-8 used?

- Customer insight and involvement: Engaging key opinion leaders who influence future practice.

- Product claims and messaging: Exploring how to tell a brand's story from multiple perspectives.

- New product/service creation: Comparing current usage and devising solutions for known (and newly discovered) problems.

- Mission and strategy articulation: Helping leaders articulate a unifying vision and big-picture direction.

How is N-of-8 different?

- It goes beyond merely "coming up with ideas," facilitating both assessment and planning to put ideas into action.

Why is N-of-8 relevant?

- Its structured approach fosters meaningful innovation, measured in tangible results, marketing differentiation, and brand clarity.

Let me give you an example of this tool used in market research. The goal of traditional focus groups is to understand what drives a target customer segment -- what they think, what they feel, and what they do. However, the goals can be more complex in health-care focus group initiatives. In real-world practice, the medical visit interaction between patient and provider is central to optimal outcomes, and is dependent on effective patient-provider dialogue. Therefore, why separate groups of physicians and patients?

I helped moderate series of N-of-8 groups about Alzheimer's Disease to better understand communications between neurologists and caregivers, including treatment discussions and disease challenges. In these groups, we uncovered that providers did not appreciate the stigma that a diagnosis meant to caregivers, in their words "a death sentence." They also got a better sense of the "secret keeping" patients used to hide symptoms, which meant caregivers were not identifying tell-tale signs. Neurologists frankly admitted they feel helpless because there are no definitive measures for disease progression. In the dialogue, the groups together concluded that "loss of identity" was something shared – patients losing their memory, caregivers losing their long-standing role in a relationship, and neurologists losing their ability to control a condition with proven diagnostics and treatments.

This application of the N-of-8 methodology underscored important lessons in patient-provider interaction.

The N-of-8 method materialized as my signature technique, transforming me into a more effective creative facilitator and strategist. It changed my approach, enabling me to meticulously identify inconsistencies in reports, reflect thoughtfully before responding, and monitor the intricate process flow of departments and clients. By asking probing questions, developing systematic methodologies, and keenly attending to details, I cultivated a heightened ability to listen to diverse perspectives. Withholding my opinions became a practice, fostering an environment where decisions, grounded in solid analysis, proved more reliable than relying solely on intuition. This method evolved into an invaluable asset, shaping my creative leadership journey.

Crafting YOUR Signature Method

Across the world of creativity, one common thread binds successful individuals—each has a unique and identifiable creative process, a signature method that drives their excellence. Through 250 interviews with creatives worldwide, this chapter explores the transformative power of cultivating your own signature method and its potential to elevate your creative endeavors.

Relying solely on inspiration is not enough. Success comes from a disciplined commitment to honing your craft. For podcasters and other creatives, this chapter emphasizes the importance of creating a signature branded method—one that acts as a compass to guide your creative journey with intention and purpose.

The chapter highlights examples from several creatives who have developed signature methods:

- Adam Alter focuses on creative problem-solving, addressing emotional, cognitive, and actionable aspects.

- Christof Zürn developed Music Thinking, a framework that uses musical terms metaphorically to foster creativity and collaboration.

- Robin Landa introduces the 3G approach. Her focus on curiosity, listening, and diverse perspectives debunks the myth that creativity cannot be taught.

- Olesija Saue explores personal branding with a focus on authenticity, passion, and strategic self-presentation.

- My Signature Method: N-of-8 Groups—a creative facilitation model designed not only to generate ideas but also to assess and plan how to execute them.

Now, you can begin to create your own signature method, capitalizing on the lessons learned from these experts:

- **Define your style:** Identify the elements that set your work apart.

- **Name your process:** Give your method a unique, memorable name.

- **Document your method:** Outline the steps and key decisions in your creative process.

- **Teach your approach:** Share your process with others through workshops or mentorship.

- **Emphasize your uniqueness:** Showcase what makes your method distinct.

- **Monetize your difference:** Understand the value of your method and turn it into a professional asset.

Developing your signature method isn't about limiting creativity but unlocking its full potential. By discovering the rituals and practices that align with your creative voice, you will leave a distinctive and meaningful mark in the world of creativity. This chapter serves as your roadmap for defining your creative compass and making your unique approach a valuable, professional asset.

Questions

1. How does the chapter highlight the role of a signature method in the creative process?

2. How does the chapter challenge the common notion that creativity is solely about spontaneity and inspiration? How does it emphasize the importance of a strong work ethic and discipline?

3. Identify examples from Adam Alter, Christof Zürn, and Robin Landa on how they established their signature methods. What was the impact on their creative endeavors?

4. What implications does the chapter suggest for you? How can you apply the lessons from Olesija Saue to create a signature branded method for your own creative work?

5. What aspects of your personal brand, both physical and digital, do you believe resonate most authentically with your values and strengths? Consider whether your strengths, values, and personal story are strategically communicated to appeal to your ideal target audience. How can you ensure that your personal brand is a genuine reflection of who you are?

6. In what ways can you leverage your personal brand to foster meaningful collaborations and authentic relationships in your creative endeavors? How can you use your personal brand to initiate discussions, both online and offline, and create authentic connections that contribute to your creative growth and success?

7. How does the chapter encourage you to document and teach your unique, named processes? How will this benefit your audiences, clients, and sponsors?

8. Reflect on my personal stories shared in the chapter. How do these stories align with the lessons about creating a signature method? What insights can you gather from my experiences in this regard?

LESSON TWO

Building a Backbone of Resilience

In the world of creativity, resilience stands as the backbone that sustains and propels the creative process forward. Across my interviews with over 250 creatives, one message emerged clearly: failure isn't an end, but rather a stepping stone to evolution and growth. This chapter explores how resilience transforms setbacks into opportunities, providing the foundation for enduring innovation and success.

Dave Noll offers a striking example, having encountered early skepticism when pitching what would become the long-running show *Chopped*. He persisted through multiple rejections, convinced of the concept's potential, and ultimately proved critics wrong. In a similar vein, Dan Klitsner refined *Bop It* after facing repeated rejection. His dedication paid off, leading to the widespread success of a now-iconic game—further amplified by his *Bop It for Good* initiative, which demonstrates how resilience can fuel social impact as well as commercial viability.

On the organizational side, Anne Jacoby emphasizes curiosity and continuous learning as central to building creative energy at every level of a company. By viewing failure as part of the process, teams become more agile and willing to experiment. Likewise, Nicholas Ind urges brands to consider their broader responsibilities to society, underlining how resilience prepares organizations to adapt and remain relevant in a rapidly changing world.

Some creatives direct their resilience toward large-scale challenges. Joni Kindwall-Moore's work with Snacktivist Foods exemplifies this determination—she challenges entrenched agricultural practices by championing ancient grains and regenerative farming, illustrating how a steadfast commitment to innovation can drive meaningful environmental change.

My own experiences with DayPro and UCB/Cimzia reflect the same essential qualities: flexibility, strategic thinking, and a willingness to pivot based on feedback. These traits have often made the difference between stalled ideas and successful campaigns. Resilience, in this sense, isn't about stubbornly pushing forward without reflection—it's about continuously adapting and improving in response to real-world conditions.

Ultimately, resilience is more than simply weathering setbacks; it's the engine that keeps creativity moving forward. By embracing new ideas, refining strategies, and maintaining a spirit of collaboration, individuals and organizations alike discover that each obstacle can lead to deeper insights and stronger outcomes. This chapter will emphasize how cultivating resilience not only helps us confront inevitable challenges but also propels our creative work to new heights.

To bring this concept to life, let's look at the experiences of innovators who continually pivot, refine, and push forward despite early roadblocks. These next stories demonstrate resilience in action, revealing how creative professionals navigate adversity to spark innovation and lasting success. From game show pitches to organizational cultures, the following examples highlight the diverse ways creatives harness resilience to transform setbacks into opportunities.

Dave Noll: 'Chopped'

Dave Noll, a creative powerhouse in the television industry, has demonstrated remarkable resilience and perseverance throughout his career, especially in developing, pitching, and producing the hit show *Chopped.* In my interview, Dave shared key moments from his journey, offering insights into how he navigated the highs and lows of the competitive world of TV production.

With a career spanning over 3,300 episodes of television programming, Dave's prolific output showcases his dedication to the industry. *Chopped* has become a cornerstone of Food Network's lineup, but the road to its success wasn't easy.

When Dave Noll first pitched *Chopped* to Food Network in 2007, he believed in its potential—but the network didn't. The show was rejected. For Dave, it was a crushing moment. He had poured his energy into crafting a unique competition format, only to hear executives say they didn't see how it would work. But instead of walking away, he regrouped.

Months later, he and his team went back to Food Network with the same concept. Even then, the battle was far from over. *Chopped* didn't just get the green light overnight—it took more than two years to make it to series. Every step was an uphill climb, filled with setbacks, doubts, and the constant need to prove the show's worth.

Much like the contestants on *Chopped*, Dave had to navigate unexpected challenges, think on his feet, and push forward despite rejection. His story is a testament to resilience—a reminder that success isn't about avoiding failure but about having the tenacity to rise each time you're knocked down.

Despite these setbacks, Dave's unwavering belief in the show and its ability to revolutionize food-based TV kept him pushing forward. He emphasizes the importance of believing in your creative vision, even when others are skeptical. His persistence eventually led to *Chopped*'s success, proving that resilience is key to bringing a bold idea to life.

A central theme in Dave's journey is his pursuit of a "forever format"—a show designed to last for decades and reach international audiences. Inspired by TV mogul Barry Diller, Dave and his creative partner, Cleve Keller, focused on creating formats that could stand the test of time. This strategic mindset played a crucial role in *Chopped*'s longevity and global reach, setting it apart from more short-lived formats. Dave explains that the key to building a "forever format" lies in simplicity, a universally appealing concept, and adaptability across different cultures.

Throughout the interview, Dave's positivity shines through. He highlights the importance of staying optimistic in pitches and creative meetings. Confidence and enthusiasm, he notes, are infectious and can help win over skeptical executives. When discussing his approach to pitching, Dave emphasizes the value of simplicity and positivity. Finding that unique "aha moment" that makes a pitch stand out is critical, and Dave has mastered the art of identifying the hook that resonates with both network executives and audiences.

Another major influence on Dave's career is his long-standing creative partnership with Cleve Keller. Dave likens their dynamic to iconic creative duos like Lennon and McCartney. Their constant exchange of ideas, open communication, and mutual respect fuel their creative process. Together, they have developed a deep understanding of what works in television, and their shared passion for innovation drives them to continually create new, successful formats. This collaboration has been vital to navigating the challenges of the television industry and maintaining a steady flow of creative output.

Dave also reflects on the enduring appeal of competition-based formats in television. From *Survivor* to *American Idol*, he sees the competitive element as timeless, resonating with audiences across generations. The success of *Chopped* is a testament to this insight, as its format taps into the excitement of competition while also highlighting creativity and culinary skills. Dave's understanding of the TV landscape and his ability to adapt to industry shifts have been key to his success.

As Dave Noll continues to contribute to the television world, his journey serves as an inspiring example of the resilience and perseverance required to turn creative visions into long-lasting success. His story offers valuable lessons for aspiring creatives and industry professionals, demonstrating that with passion, positivity, and determination, even the most ambitious creative ideas can become reality.

Dan Klitsner: *Bop-It*

Dan Klitsner, the inventor of *Bop-It*, was a memorable guest on the *Unlocking Your World of Creativity* podcast, where we discussed his journey in inventing, pitching, and evolving *Bop-It* over the years. Our conversation ranged from the creative process to the art of pitching, and the many iterations of the *Bop-It* game that followed its original success.

Dan began his career as an industrial designer, with a focus on creating products that were both ergonomic and problem-solving. His unique approach to game design centered around the concept of "animating the player" rather than the game itself. This philosophy was key in the creation of *Bop-It*, a game that instructs players to perform physical actions like bopping, twisting, and pulling. The idea was simple yet innovative—it turned the player into the focus of the game's action.

The first prototype of *Bop-It* was a foamcore handheld model, which Dan used to pitch the concept to potential partners. Despite his passion for the idea, the initial pitches were met with resistance, as some executives struggled to see its potential. One particular moment of rejection occurred when a key pitch fell flat, with the executives dismissing the game as too simple. However, Dan's belief in the concept kept him going. He took the feedback, refined the game, and eventually found a partner who saw the potential. His persistence paid off.

Bop-It became a cultural phenomenon.

Following the success of *Bop-It*, Dan expanded the concept with new iterations, including *Bop-It Extreme* and later variations like *Bop-It Tetris* and *Bop-It Smash*. Each iteration built upon his core idea of "animating the player" in new and inventive ways. This philosophy of engaging the player physically and emotionally has continued to influence his approach to game design, pushing the boundaries of how players interact with games.

As the 25th anniversary of *Bop-It* approached, Dan decided to celebrate the milestone with a book titled *Take This Book and Bop It*. The book features a functional *Bop-It* button on the cover and dives into Dan's creative process and the story behind the invention of *Bop-It*. To commemorate the anniversary, he also launched a new product, the *Bop-It Button*. This one-button game serves as a playful nod to the original *Bop-It* and includes hidden surprises and references to the classic game, delighting long-time fans with its nostalgic appeal.

Dan's commitment to using his creativity for good is exemplified in his initiative, *Bop-It for Good*. This project aims to give back to underserved communities by donating *Bop-It* games and supporting creativity programs for children. Through this initiative, Dan demonstrates that innovation and creativity can have a meaningful social impact. By connecting his game with charitable efforts, he shows how creative work can extend beyond entertainment to make a positive difference in people's lives.

Throughout our interview, Dan shared invaluable insights into the importance of listening and adapting ideas, as well as the art of keeping pitches loose and engaging. His passion for creativity, games, and connecting with people was evident as he reflected on the lasting impact of *Bop-It* over the years.

Dan Klitsner's journey with *Bop-It* is a testament to resilience, adaptability, and a commitment to bringing joy and connection through his creative innovations. I later visited Dan's studio in downtown San Francisco, where I gained a fascinating glimpse into the mind of a prolific toy inventor and the evolution of a game that has become a cultural touchstone.

Anne Jacoby: 'Creativity Culture Guide'

In my engaging interview with Anne Jacoby, CEO of Spring Street Solutions, she shared her insights on fostering creativity, cultivating it within the workplace, and adapting to the evolving dynamics of today's world of work.

Anne's journey from the world of performing arts to the business realm shaped her unique perspective on creativity. Initially, she saw her background in theater as a potential liability in corporate settings, but she quickly realized that her creative roots were a strength. The skills she developed in the arts—storytelling, improvisation, and collaboration—became key tools in helping organizations embrace creativity as a central part of their culture.

Creativity, she argues, isn't just for artists; it's an essential element of business success.

A central theme of our conversation was the role of storytelling in shaping organizational culture. Anne stresses the importance of aligning purpose and values with behaviors, and how organizations must actively live these principles to inspire creativity. Her *Creativity Culture Guide* provides a roadmap for companies to engage their teams and activate their creative potential. This guide offers practical steps to cultivate a creative environment, such as encouraging cross-departmental collaboration and establishing regular brainstorming sessions to stimulate new ideas. One key takeaway is that creativity should not be confined to departments like marketing or design—it should permeate every corner of an organization.

Anne also highlights the importance of psychological safety within teams. Creativity thrives when individuals feel safe to share ideas without fear of judgment. For example, in a tech company she worked with, anonymous brainstorming sessions led to a breakthrough idea that wouldn't have surfaced in a more traditional, hierarchical environment. This approach enabled team members to share bold, unfiltered ideas, fostering a culture of trust and experimentation. Psychological safety, Anne explains, is essential for encouraging innovation at every level of an organization.

Our discussion also touched on connection and belonging, which are vital in building a creative and supportive community within an organization. Anne emphasizes that creativity flourishes when people feel connected to both their colleagues and the purpose of the organization. She provides actionable strategies for cultivating this connection, such as creating mentorship programs and facilitating informal gatherings where employees can share personal stories and experiences.

As our interview unfolded, Anne addressed the challenges and opportunities posed by the evolving world of work, especially with the rise of remote and hybrid models. She sees creativity as a key differentiator for organizations looking to build unique cultures that attract and retain talent. Drawing from her *Creativity Culture Guide*, Anne shares practical steps for fostering creativity in this new landscape. She advocates for continuous listening and feedback loops to ensure that companies understand the needs and desires of their employees, adapting their strategies accordingly.

Anne also discussed how technology can support creativity and inclusivity. Tools that enable anonymous idea sharing or virtual collaboration can help break down biases and ensure that diverse voices are heard. In one organization, the use of anonymous feedback forms led to a flood of new ideas from employees who had previously been reluctant to speak up in meetings. This kind of inclusion, Anne suggests, is critical for fostering a diverse and creative workplace.

The conversation concluded with Anne expressing her passion for collaboration and her openness to connecting with others. She encourages listeners to reach out, stressing the power of diverse perspectives and experiences in driving creativity forward.

Nicholas Ind: 'Brands with a Conscience'

Another insightful interview was with Nicholas Ind, a professor at Christiana University College in Oslo, Norway, with a background in design and branding consultancy. Nicholas bridges the gap between theoretical approaches to creativity and its practical application in business. During our conversation, he discussed two of his recent books, *Co-Creating Brands* and *Brands with a Conscience*, which explore the principles of building brands collaboratively and showcase case studies of organizations that prioritize transparency and social responsibility.

In *Brands with a Conscience*, Nicholas highlights companies that align their brand with ethical principles, making a positive impact on society and the environment. For example, Patagonia, the outdoor clothing brand, embodies these ideals by integrating sustainability into every facet of its business. The company not only creates eco-friendly products but also actively advocates for environmental protection, embodying the idea that brands can be a force for good. This case study illustrates the core message of *Brands with a Conscience*—that businesses should prioritize their responsibility to customers, employees, and society at large.

Nicholas is part of a collective think tank that encourages brand owners to consider their broader responsibility beyond just serving customers. The conversation examined his creative process, particularly the importance of collaboration, seeking diverse perspectives, and maintaining a willingness to be vulnerable. Drawing from his experience in both academia and business, Nicholas stressed the need for resilience and adaptability in long-term planning. These traits are crucial for navigating the evolving business landscape, where balancing profit with ethical considerations is becoming increasingly important.

A significant shift in recent years, accelerated by the COVID-19 pandemic, has been the transition from a focus on individualism ("me") to a more collective approach ("we"). Nicholas observes that businesses are moving from shareholder primacy toward a stakeholder perspective, where they recognize the interconnectedness of their customers, employees, suppliers, and communities. Creativity plays a central role in fostering this innovation, but Nicholas acknowledges the challenges of implementing creative ideas within organizations. He speaks to the tension between the desire for fast-moving, innovative initiatives and the bureaucratic structures that often slow down progress.

For instance, in one case study, a global corporation attempted to implement a series of sustainability initiatives, but these were bogged down by internal resistance from multiple departments. Nicholas suggests strategies for overcoming this friction, including involving key stakeholders early in the process, ensuring that creative ideas are aligned with business relevance, and in some cases, establishing innovation labs that allow for more agile, creative problem-solving outside the constraints of standard bureaucracy.

The conversation also touched on the implications of these ideas for individual artists. Nicholas highlights the value of social connection and staying aware of the world around them. He advises artists to draw inspiration from others and remain open to new ideas, noting that even the smallest nugget of information can spark a creative breakthrough. For example, he describes how one artist found inspiration for a large-scale installation from observing something as simple as a conversation between two strangers. This underscores the importance of remaining open to diverse perspectives and being connected to the broader social environment.

As organizations and individuals alike navigate a world where social responsibility, creativity, and adaptability are paramount, Nicholas Ind's insights provide a valuable roadmap for fostering meaningful innovation while staying true to ethical principles.

Joni Kindwall-Moore: Snacktivist Foods

Joni Kindwall-Moore, founder of Snacktivist Foods, is on a mission to revolutionize the food system by embracing regenerative agriculture and challenging well-established industry processes. Her company, based in Northern Idaho, is both women-owned and Mom-owned, and it leads the charge in creating a new grain economy with its innovative baking mixes and finished products. Snacktivist's offerings—vegan, gluten-free, non-GMO, and whole grain—stand out in a crowded market. As Joni puts it, "Our mantra is that it's what we put in our products that is exceptional, not what we leave out."

Snacktivist Foods uses superfood ancient grains and legumes such as millet, teff, sorghum, and ancient wheat—ingredients that have nourished humans for thousands of years but have been largely forgotten by modern agriculture. Joni explains that these nutrient-dense, hardy grains are central to the regenerative agriculture movement, a farming method that emphasizes restoring and maintaining soil health. "Regenerative agriculture has the potential to help restore the world's soils, making them more drought-resistant, disease-resistant, and less dependent on chemical inputs," Joni says.

Taking on the established food industry, with its reliance on conventional supply chains and multinational corporations, posed significant challenges for Joni and her team. She faced resistance from large suppliers and had to navigate the complexities of sourcing lesser-known grains from sustainable, small-scale farms. However, Joni's commitment to reshaping the food system, from the ground up, kept her pushing forward. Her resilience in the face of these obstacles reflects Snacktivist's core belief that changing the food system is not just possible—it's necessary.

At the heart of Joni's vision is a belief that regenerative farming doesn't just produce healthier food—it also plays a critical role in combating climate change. Regenerative agriculture, she explains, fosters biodiversity in farmlands and improves soil health by sequestering carbon, reducing the need for harmful chemical inputs, and making land more resilient to drought and disease. "We believe that this agro-ecological method of farming creates biodiversity in our farmlands," Joni says, adding that it's a method that can help put carbon back into the Earth's crust, reduce pollution, and conserve water. Through these practices, regenerative farming supports the fight against climate change.

Snacktivist's innovative approach to using ancient grains goes beyond offering better-for-you baked goods—it helps create a new economic model that supports both environmental sustainability and social responsibility. Joni's vision is not only about producing healthy, sustainable food but also about advocating for a new grain economy that benefits both farmers and consumers. "We are helping to save the planet, one waffle at a time!" Joni cheers.

This blend of ecological purpose and product innovation has helped Snacktivist carve out a niche in the food industry. By focusing on what's included in their products—nutrient-dense, sustainably sourced grains—Snacktivist offers a fresh take on the "better-for-you" food movement, setting them apart from competitors who often emphasize what they leave out.

As Joni continues to push Snacktivist Foods forward, her commitment to sustainability and regenerative farming serves as a powerful example of how small companies can drive significant change. Her journey is one of resilience, innovation, and a deep belief in the power of food to reshape the world for the better.

***

As I reflect on the incredible stories of resilience from creative professionals like Dave Noll, Dan Klitsner, Anne Jacoby, Joni Kindwall-Moore, and Nicholas Ind, I'm reminded of the invaluable lessons their experiences have taught me. Their determination to push through setbacks and their ability to adapt to changing circumstances provide profound insights into what it means to stay committed to creative goals, no matter the challenges that arise.

Looking back on my own career, I feel a deep sense of gratitude for the opportunities I've had to navigate the highs and lows of the creative journey. There were moments of excitement when ideas took flight, and times of uncertainty when projects seemed on the verge of collapse. Through it all, I've learned that resilience is not just a skill, but a way of thinking—a mindset that allows you to turn obstacles into stepping stones, much like the people whose stories I've shared.

As I transition into my own experiences, I hope to offer a personal reflection on the importance of resilience in my journey. These stories are reminders that the lessons I've learned through both triumphs and setbacks may resonate with others who find themselves in the midst of their own creative struggles. By sharing these insights, I aim to help others see that resilience, adaptability, and persistence are the true pillars of a lasting, successful creative career. Whether you're just starting out or looking for ways to reinvigorate your approach, my hope is that these personal experiences will inspire and empower you to keep moving forward, no matter what challenges come your way.

My Experience with DAYPRO

My marketing experience with DayPro, the arthritis drug, presented a unique challenge—one that required not just strong clinical data but also a compelling brand narrative. Market analysis revealed a major obstacle: DayPro was one of three similar drugs, lacking any distinct positioning. It had no story to set it apart.

Determined to change that, I collaborated with a skilled medical writer to dive deep into the clinical literature. That's where we uncovered a critical insight—DayPro had a unique ability to self-regulate its buildup, preventing excessive accumulation in the body. We named this phenomenon "compensatory clearance," transforming it into the focal point of our rebranding strategy. What had once been an undifferentiated product now had a powerful, science-backed advantage that reshaped its market perception.

With this discovery, we shifted our focus from the old positioning DayPro as a reactive treatment to marketing it as a daily preventive measure against arthritis pain. Our tagline, "Daylong

Confidence, Proactive Intervention," captured the essence of this new approach. The branding strategy emphasized DayPro's reliability for long-term use, appealing to patients who wanted to manage their arthritis before pain became debilitating.

The results were transformative. Over the next three years, we reversed the drug's market share decline and saw a remarkable 20% boost in sales. This success was a testament to the power of combining scientific insight with a clear, forward-thinking brand strategy.

However, the journey wasn't without its challenges. One major hurdle came in navigating team dynamics and client relationships. There were moments of friction—particularly when our bold rebranding strategy faced internal skepticism. Some stakeholders hesitated to embrace the shift from a well-established positioning to a more proactive approach. Convincing the team to trust in the new direction required not only resilience but also a blend of diplomacy and tenacity. I had to ensure that I remained both enthusiastic and persuasive, while also addressing concerns with empathy and clarity.

Personally, the process challenged me to maintain high levels of energy and enthusiasm while balancing the complex dynamics at play. As someone who thrives on progress and accomplishment, I had to be mindful of pacing myself—keeping the project's momentum going while ensuring I didn't burn out or dismiss others' concerns along the way. Striking that balance was crucial to staying resilient and focused on the bigger picture.

The experience also highlighted the importance of adaptability in leadership. While I naturally enjoy building rapport and maintaining positive relationships, this project taught me the value of acknowledging the negative aspects of any situation without letting them detract from the overall vision. It wasn't just about being agreeable—it was about steering the team with confidence, even when faced with resistance.

In the world of brand innovation, every scientific breakthrough, no matter how robust, requires a human touch to translate it into a compelling story for consumers. My time with DayPro taught me that resilience is more than just overcoming obstacles; it's about adapting my leadership and communication style to fit the challenges at hand. With a combination of enthusiasm, strategic thinking, and an unwavering commitment to excellence, we successfully transformed DayPro from a standard treatment into a daily companion in the fight against arthritis. The journey proved the incredible power of brand innovation, guided by resilience and adaptability, to drive meaningful change.

My Involvement with Acromegaly

In the pharmaceutical industry, the journey from drug development to market approval is often filled with uncertainties. My experience with Endo Pharmaceuticals Holding Inc. exemplified the resilience, creativity, and adaptability required to navigate these challenges—particularly during the market research phase for a novel drug targeting acromegaly, a condition characterized by the overproduction of growth hormone, leading to abnormal growth of the hands and feet.

From the start, the project presented inherent complexities. We were working on an implant designed to treat this rare condition, but as with any drug under FDA review, the pressure was immense, and the timelines were tight. One of the biggest challenges came when the FDA unexpectedly requested additional animal studies, including a carcinogenicity study. This added a new layer of complexity and delayed the process significantly. The abruptness of this request forced us to pivot, and the eventual decision to discontinue the drug's development was a tough pill to swallow. It underscored the unpredictable nature of drug development, where even the best-laid plans can be derailed by unexpected regulatory requirements.

Throughout this journey, my tendency to say "yes" to new challenges was both a strength and a difficulty. I often found myself agreeing to high-pressure demands, driven by the urgency of the FDA review process. There was little room for routine or detailed planning, which required me to focus on immediate priorities and adapt to the ever-shifting landscape of pharmaceutical development. I learned the value of maintaining focus while navigating these challenges, balancing the intense demands with a creative and flexible approach to problem-solving.

Despite the setbacks, my passion for exploring unconventional avenues of market research proved invaluable. The acromegaly treatment landscape is highly specialized, and traditional research methods didn't always provide the insights we needed. By embracing creativity, I explored new ways to gather data and insights that hadn't been previously considered. For instance, I looked beyond standard patient profiles and engaged with advocacy groups and niche medical communities, which provided a deeper understanding of patient needs and market gaps. This willingness to think outside the box became critical in adapting our strategies to the evolving circumstances of the project.

My positive approach to the work was crucial during this challenging time. Navigating the uncertainties of FDA reviews and the eventual decision to halt the drug's development was emotionally taxing for the entire team. However, my ability to remain optimistic and foster a supportive environment helped maintain team morale. I focused on creating a work atmosphere that was both welcoming and energizing, encouraging everyone to push forward even in the face of disappointment. This collective resilience became a cornerstone for keeping the project on track until we reached the final decision to halt development.

While the decision to discontinue development was disappointing, it also presented an opportunity for reflection. It reminded me that the pharmaceutical landscape is always changing, and resilience isn't just about weathering setbacks—it's about continuously adapting and looking for new paths forward. Even though we didn't reach the finish line with this particular treatment, the insights gained and the creative strategies we employed will undoubtedly influence future projects.

My experience with Endo reinforced a vital lesson: in the complex world of drug development, resilience and creativity are not optional—they are essential. Even when faced with unexpected turns and setbacks, the ability to stay focused on long-term goals, pivot creatively, and foster team spirit is what drives success.

Client Issues for Lilly/Axid

As a seasoned professional in advertising, I've faced my share of challenges. However, a particular client confrontation during a project for Lilly/Axid tested my resilience like never before, revealing both my strengths and areas where I could grow. The situation arose when Lilly, one of our major pharmaceutical clients, raised serious concerns about our quality control processes, particularly in the areas of fact-checking and referencing in our deliverables. The errors threatened the integrity of our campaign and our reputation as an agency. The client's dissatisfaction was clear, and they demanded immediate solutions.

It wasn't just a moment for damage control—it required a looking closely into our internal processes, an honest assessment of where things had gone wrong, and a commitment to fix those issues at their core.

Looking back, there were key strengths that helped navigate this difficult situation. One of my most valuable assets was the ability to use intuition to uncover hidden issues that weren't immediately apparent. While the client initially pointed to errors in documentation, I probed deeper and discovered that the root cause stemmed from a lack of clarity in our internal communication and cross-team coordination. Fixing these underlying problems not only addressed the client's concerns but also improved our overall workflow.

My natural ability to build rapport also played a crucial role. In the midst of heightened tension, I focused on creating a calm and open environment for dialogue with the client. By doing so, we were able to move past the initial frustration and have a constructive conversation about how we could meet their expectations. This openness paved the way for a more collaborative approach to solving the problem.

Quick thinking in response to the client's questions was another strength that became essential during this crisis. Rather than becoming defensive or evasive, I responded directly and transparently to their concerns. This immediate engagement helped restore the client's trust and demonstrated our commitment to taking their feedback seriously.

Maintaining a sense of equity and collaboration was critical. I recognized that preserving a harmonious relationship with Lilly was just as important as addressing their concerns. By ensuring that we worked together as partners rather than engaging in a blame game, we could focus on finding solutions that worked for both sides.

In my responses, I found that appealing to both logical and emotional motives was highly effective. On the one hand, I laid out a data-driven plan for how we would correct the quality control issues and prevent future mistakes. On the other hand, I acknowledged the emotional toll that the errors had taken on the client, showing empathy for the stress and frustration they were experiencing.

In retrospect, I can see areas where I could have improved. For one, I realized that I tended to take client objections at face value rather than probing deeper into their concerns from the outset. Had I dug into the root causes earlier, we might have addressed the underlying issues before they escalated. Additionally, taking time to recap areas of agreement might have balanced the conversation, allowing us to highlight what was working well even amid the crisis.

Another valuable lesson was the importance of clarifying doubts fully before rushing to solutions. In our eagerness to fix the situation, there were moments when we moved too quickly, without fully understanding the client's expectations. Taking a step back to ensure clarity could have streamlined the resolution process and prevented some miscommunications.

One of the hardest lessons I learned was not to take rejection personally. When a major client like Lilly expresses dissatisfaction, it's easy to internalize that as a personal failure. Over time, I've come to understand that client feedback is part of the professional journey, and the best way to respond is by focusing on rectifying the situation rather than dwelling on the emotional impact.

Finally, I've learned the importance of persisting through tough issues until they are fully resolved. While it's tempting to prioritize a quick fix, addressing the deeper, more complex problems ensures long-term client satisfaction. Moving forward, I've embraced the idea that a thorough resolution process, even if it takes more time, is ultimately what strengthens client relationships.

In conclusion, this confrontation with Lilly/Axid was a defining moment in my career, one that forced me to re-examine how I handle adversity, build resilience, and continually improve. By addressing both my strengths and areas for growth, I came away from this experience with a renewed commitment to excellence and a better understanding of what it takes to succeed in client relationships. The lessons I learned during this project have since become a cornerstone of how I approach challenges—embracing both the logical and emotional aspects of problem-solving, while continuously striving for improvement.

Lesson Learned on the Pitch for UCB/Cimzia

Embarking on an agency pitch is always a rollercoaster ride filled with highs, lows, and unexpected twists. My experience with the UCB Cimzia pitch was no different, and it illuminated the importance of personal creative skills in navigating this intricate process. The lessons I learned from this pitch still resonate with me today, influencing how I approach each new opportunity.

From the outset, I realized that asking the right questions was critical to understanding the brand team's true needs. Rather than assuming we understood the scope, I pushed myself to dig deeper, asking follow-up questions that revealed insights we would have otherwise missed. For example, I discovered a key concern about the brand's positioning in a crowded market, which allowed us to adjust our pitch to address those specific needs. Summarizing benefits concisely became an art—highlighting the agency's strengths while avoiding the temptation to overpromise or overwhelm the client with too much information.

One important lesson was the value of reviewing agreed-upon points before moving forward. As the pitch progressed, I made sure we revisited key takeaways from each conversation, ensuring that we and the client were always on the same page. At the same time, I had to be careful to rein in my enthusiasm—it's easy to get carried away with one solution and inadvertently overshadow other potential options. By staying balanced and open to feedback, we were able to present a broader, more versatile strategy that resonated with the client.

However, the post-pitch phase came with its own set of challenges. As feedback from the client rolled in, we had to pivot quickly, addressing concerns while maintaining the momentum of the original pitch. One of the most valuable pieces of feedback we received was about the depth of our research. While the client appreciated our strategic approach, they felt we could have dived deeper into the specific pain points of Cimzia's audience. Taking this to heart, we refined our follow-up presentations to better align with their expectations, ultimately strengthening our position.

This phase also taught me the importance of asking for written referrals and testimonials—a step I had often overlooked in the past. Having these in hand not only helps build credibility but also provides a tangible record of client satisfaction that can be leveraged in future pitches. Additionally, I learned the necessity of agreeing on clear next steps with the client. Too often, pitches end with a vague sense of what comes next. This time, I made sure we had concrete follow-up actions in place, including timelines and deliverables, which kept the process moving forward smoothly.

One key realization during the post-pitch phase was that not all follow-up calls are simply polite check-ins—they are critical to maintaining momentum and deepening the relationship with the client. During one follow-up call, I learned that the client's internal priorities had shifted slightly, which allowed us to tweak our approach and stay relevant to their evolving needs. Patience became another important lesson, as I recognized that some clients needed time to reflect before making a decision. Rather than pushing for immediate answers, I focused on staying present and available, giving them the space to make an informed choice.

The UCB Cimzia pitch taught me that the agency pitch process requires a blend of creativity, strategic thinking, and adaptability at every step. From crafting the perfect initial pitch to navigating the complexities of client feedback and follow-up, each phase demands a different set of skills. Ultimately, the pitch process is not just about winning business—it's about building trust, demonstrating value, and forging long-term relationships with clients.

Resilience as YOUR Creative Backbone

In the world of creativity and innovation, learning from mistakes and adapting to achieve goals is crucial. This lesson highlights the importance of developing contingency plans and staying resilient in the face of unforeseen challenges. The key is to anticipate obstacles and create backup ideas to navigate difficulties successfully, while also maintaining a mindset of adaptability and continuous learning.

- Dave Noll demonstrated remarkable resilience in developing *Chopped*, a show that faced significant challenges during its pitch and development stages. Despite early skepticism, Dave's belief in the concept never wavered. His persistence paid off, turning *Chopped* into a cornerstone of the Food Network's programming and underscoring the power of staying committed to creative ideas, even when faced with initial rejection.

- Dan Klitsner's *Bop-It* innovation is another example of resilience in action. After facing rejection during its early stages, Dan adapted and refined the game until it gained acceptance. The 25th anniversary of *Bop-It* reflects ongoing innovation, including the *Bop-It for Good* initiative, which combines creativity with a mission to give back. Dan's journey shows how embracing feedback and persistence can lead to long-term success.

- Anne Jacoby emphasizes the importance of tapping into curiosity and learning as a source of creative energy. In her work, storytelling is key to shaping organizational culture and activating creative potential. Anne challenges the idea that creativity is limited to certain departments, encouraging companies to foster a creative mindset across all areas to inspire innovation and ingenuity.

- Joni Kindwall-Moore's Snacktivist Foods is transforming the food system by embracing regenerative agriculture. By utilizing ancient grains and legumes, Joni is creating a new grain economy that promotes biodiversity and sustainability. Her resilience in tackling well-established agricultural practices and multinational corporations shows how creative thinking can be applied to solve some of the world's most pressing environmental issues. Joni's mission to "save the planet, one waffle at a time" captures the essence of her long-term vision.

- Nicholas Ind highlights the need for brands to consider their responsibilities to stakeholders and society at large. His work encourages a shift from individualism to a more collective approach, where businesses act as positive forces for change. He also emphasizes the value of creativity in overcoming bureaucratic challenges within organizations and stresses the importance of social connection and openness to different ideas for individual artists.

- My personal experiences in resilience and adaptability, such as the DayPro campaign and Endo acromegaly drug development, further illustrate the importance of creative problem-solving and flexibility. Navigating complex team and client dynamics required a blend of enthusiasm, strategic thinking, and team spirit. Similarly, in the UCB/ Cimzia pitch, asking the right questions, summarizing key benefits, and agreeing on next steps were critical in gaining commitment from the brand team. These experiences taught me the value of patience, adaptability, and the importance of understanding evolving client needs.

These stories from creative professionals underline the universal importance of resilience, adaptability, and continuous learning in achieving creative goals. Each narrative highlights how anticipating challenges, developing contingency plans, and maintaining a positive, innovative mindset are essential for navigating the highs and lows of the creative journey.

In the following key takeaways, we distill essential lessons from these examples to guide you in shaping your own resilient approach to creative pursuits—paving the way for our next chapter, where we'll explore how collaboration amplifies these core principles and drives innovative outcomes.

Key Takeaways

- **Anticipate setbacks:** Develop contingency plans that allow for flexibility and creativity when unexpected challenges arise.

- **Stay committed to your vision:** Even when faced with skepticism or setbacks, persistence and belief in your creative ideas are key to long-term success.

- **Embrace adaptability:** Being willing to pivot and adjust strategies based on feedback or changing circumstances is essential for thriving in creative fields.

- **Foster a creative mindset across all areas:** Creativity should not be confined to certain roles or departments—every part of an organization can contribute to innovation.

Questions

1. Have you encountered failure or rejection in your creative pursuits like Dave Noll, and if so, how did you react to it?

2. Reflecting on the experiences of game show creator Dave Noll and Dan Klitsner of *Bop-it*, how do you perceive the role of resilience in driving creative fulfillment?

3. Consider instances in your own creative journey where you've faced challenges. How did resilience play a role in your ability to overcome obstacles and continue pursuing your artistic goals?

4. In what ways have you embraced failure as an integral part of the creative process, and how has it contributed to your personal and artistic growth?

5. Drawing from the examples in the chapter, how can the mindset of "not taking no for an answer" and learning from mistakes be applied to your creative endeavors?

6. Reflect on your attitude towards failure. Do you see it as an opportunity to learn and grow, or do you tend to fear

and avoid it? How might shifting this perspective impact your creative process?

7. How can you tap into your curiosity and passion for learning to fuel your creative energy in your professional or creative pursuits, considering Anne Jacoby's emphasis on these sources of inspiration?

8. In light of Anne's assertion that creativity is a mindset that should extend across all parts of an organization, how can you contribute to fostering a culture of creativity and innovation within your team or workplace, regardless of your role or department?

9. Ask yourself: "How willing am I to collaborate with diverse perspectives, be vulnerable in sharing my ideas, and actively involve key stakeholders in the creative processes of my projects?"

10. Reflecting on your work in light of Nicholas' approach, ask: "In my professional or creative endeavors, have I considered the shift from an individualistic ("me") approach to a more collective ("we") perspective, acknowledging the interconnectedness of various stakeholders?"

11. How can you apply lessons from Mark's projects?

LESSON THREE

Partnering with Collaborators

Throughout my creative journey, collaboration has been a cornerstone of everything I do. The ability to bring together individuals with unique perspectives, complementary skills, and shared visions has transformed not only projects but entire creative careers—including my own. This lesson celebrates collaboration's transformative power and its role in fostering innovation, growth, and creative breakthroughs that are impossible to achieve alone.

Diverse Perspectives and Shared Visions

The art of collaboration takes many forms. Whether it's a creative partnership between peers, the dynamic relationship between leaders and their teams, or the fusion of ideas across disciplines, working together opens up new opportunities for innovation. This chapter explores how diverse voices spark powerful outcomes, drawing on stories of industry leaders and my own experiences:

- **Vinnie Potestivo (Former MTV Executive):** Vinnie explains how teamwork fueled the creation of hit shows like *Cribs.* He discusses the transition from traditional television to online interactive content and offers practical advice on pursuing awards and strategically releasing content for maximum visibility.

- **Michael Robinson (International Hotel Manager):** Michael highlights the importance of creativity in hospitality and shows how aligning creative initiatives with business goals can enhance the guest experience. His examples—from weaving local culture into hotel offerings to launching post-COVID bar takeovers—demonstrate how bold thinking and collaboration keep the hospitality industry fresh.

- **Craig Dobbin (Composer, NCIS: LA):** Craig underscores the essential role of collaboration in TV and film music. By adapting to producers' visions, he ensures his soundtracks complement each show's tone. He encourages creatives to persevere, continue sharing their work, and remain open to collaborative input.

- **José Vieira (Third-Gen. Owner, Viarco Pencil Co.):** José revitalized his family business by combining traditional craftsmanship with modern technology. Through artist residencies and creative partnerships, Viarco remains competitive in a global market, proving that collaboration across disciplines can breathe new life into longstanding brands.

- **Brian Grazer (Author, Face to Face):** Brian highlights how genuine, in-person interactions foster trust and creative synergy. His perspective underscores the importance of listening, openness, and vulnerability in forming meaningful connections that spur innovative thinking.

- **My Collaborative Experiences (RELISTOR, Baxter Global Oncology, Hollister Global Branding):** In my own work, bringing together diverse talents—whether across cultures or disciplines—proved pivotal for balancing creative imagination with analytical strategy. These experiences illustrate how cross- cultural collaboration and varied perspectives can boost both creative impact and global market success.

Navigating Challenges

While collaboration offers countless benefits, it also comes with challenges. Creative conflicts, differing visions, and coordinating efforts across industries or time zones all demand adaptability and clear communication. Reflecting on moments when collaboration could have been even more effective highlights the need to address pitfalls early—managing egos, aligning goals, and ensuring each team member's voice is heard.

Ultimately, collaboration is more than a tool—it's a mindset. By celebrating shared visions and adapting to creative tensions, we discover that no creative journey needs to be taken alone. In the pages ahead, we'll see how collaborative energy can lift projects to new heights, transforming individual ideas into collective triumphs that make a lasting impact.

Vinnie Potestivo: Personal Branding

Vinnie Potestivo emphasizes the transformative role of collaboration in the creative process and how it accelerates artistic growth. Drawing on his experiences at MTV in the early 2000s, Vinnie reflects on the collaborative work behind creating shows like *Cribs*. He recalls how teamwork between producers, editors, and talent allowed the show's guests to transition into hosts, revealing personal aspects of their lives in an authentic way.

This shift from traditional guest roles to more dynamic, personal storytelling was possible because of the collaborative environment MTV fostered, where creative minds were encouraged to share ideas freely. The success of *Cribs* and other shows was a direct result of this synergy.

Vinnie also discusses the evolution of storytelling in television as social media and platforms like YouTube gained prominence. He highlights how this shift from scripted content to more interactive and personal formats allowed audiences to connect with a broader range of personalities. Vinnie credits this evolution to the collaboration between networks, creators, and audiences, who co-created content that reflected real, diverse experiences. For example, Vinnie recounts how audience feedback directly influenced the direction of certain MTV projects, further emphasizing the importance of collaboration in content creation.

A significant point Vinnie makes is the importance of seeking recognition through awards. He reflects on his Emmy win and how it opened doors for more opportunities, from increased press coverage to enhanced search engine optimization (SEO). Vinnie advises creators to actively seek out awards and credits to strengthen their personal brand. For instance, he encourages creators to list their credits on platforms like IMDb and use award nominations and wins to boost their visibility. By strategically timing the announcement of award wins—such as during product launches or new podcast episodes—creatives can maximize the impact on their personal brand and increase discoverability.

Adaptability is another major theme in Vinnie's approach to creative success. He shares his decision to shift from a weekly podcast format to daily episodes, recognizing that timing is crucial in releasing content that resonates with audiences. Vinnie suggests that creators can enhance their visibility by releasing episodes shortly after influencers or popular figures post content, effectively riding the wave of audience engagement. By aligning their releases with existing trends or influencer content, creators can boost their chances of being discovered by new listeners.

Beyond content creation, Vinnie explains that collaboration also involves building the right team. He urges solo creators to assemble a team that complements their skill set and brings in new perspectives. Vinnie shares examples from his time at MTV, where diverse teams of individuals with varying strengths—such as editing, production, and writing—helped elevate projects. He believes that different personalities and skills can contribute unique perspectives that drive creativity forward. By fostering a collaborative environment that values each team member's input, creators can achieve greater long-term success and sustain career growth.

Michael Robinson: International Hospitality Executive

Michael Robinson, a seasoned hotel manager with a global career, shares valuable insights on creativity, leadership, and crafting superior guest experiences in luxury hotels and resorts. Having managed properties in diverse locations such as La Jolla, Dubai, Saigon, and currently Siem Reap, Cambodia, Robinson brings a wealth of international experience to the conversation.

In the interview, Robinson highlights the critical role of creativity in hospitality, particularly in the evolving landscape shaped by the COVID-19 pandemic. He acknowledges that the pandemic imposed significant financial constraints, making it more challenging to implement creative ideas. However, Robinson emphasizes the importance of aligning creative initiatives with strategic business goals to ensure that innovations not only enhance guest experiences but also generate tangible business results. For example, Robinson recalls how a limited-budget renovation of the hotel's outdoor area, coupled with strategic event planning, led to a significant boost in revenue from local visitors, demonstrating the financial impact of well-thought-out creative solutions.

Robinson finds inspiration through exercise, particularly running, which he credits with sparking creative solutions to challenges in his professional life. He notes that some of his best ideas—such as a redesigned service model for guest check-ins—came to him during morning runs. This connection between physical well-being and mental creativity underscores Robinson's holistic approach to leadership, where maintaining personal balance fuels professional success.

A cornerstone of Robinson's hospitality philosophy is his focus on local and cultural elements. He believes that integrating authentic local experiences into the guest experience enriches their stay and fosters a deeper connection to the destination. While managing a property in Vietnam, Robinson worked closely with local chefs and cultural experts to introduce a live station for making traditional Vietnamese bánh mì. This interactive experience not only delighted guests but also showcased the culinary traditions of the region, providing an immersive cultural connection. Robinson's ability to partner with local artisans to create such experiences highlights his commitment to supporting local communities and integrating their stories into the guest experience.

At FCC Angkor in Siem Reap, Robinson introduced a unique promotional concept to foster community engagement. Every Wednesday night, he personally took over the bar, allowing guests to choose the price of their cocktails. This innovative and interactive approach created a social buzz, attracting both local residents and hotel guests. The initiative led to an increase in bar revenue and cemented FCC Angkor as a key player in Siem Reap's nightlife scene. Robinson's hands-on involvement in these creative promotions exemplifies his leadership by example, building rapport with both staff and guests.

Robinson's leadership style is deeply collaborative and approachable. He encourages an open dialogue with both his team and guests, ensuring that everyone feels heard and valued. By actively participating in day-to-day operations, Robinson not only enhances the guest experience but also strengthens his relationship with his staff, creating a culture of mutual respect and creativity. His ability to step into various roles—whether behind the bar or guiding a brainstorming session—demonstrates his commitment to building a strong, engaged team.

In summary, Michael Robinson's approach to hospitality combines creativity, adaptability, and a deep appreciation for local culture. His insights demonstrate how creative thinking, even in the face of financial challenges, can elevate guest experiences and drive business results. For professionals in hospitality and beyond, Robinson's philosophy serves as a blueprint for balancing innovation with practicality, while cultivating leadership through collaboration and creativity.

Craig Dobbin: TV/Film Music Composer

In my conversation with Craig Dobbin, a renowned TV/Film music composer, we delved into his extensive work on *NCIS: LA* and his collaborations across the industry. Dobbin's contributions to the *NCIS: LA* soundtrack are iconic, and as the show nears its end, he reflected on how he has kept the music fresh and relevant throughout the series.

Dobbin joined *NCIS: LA* during its eighth season, stepping into a fast-paced, established production. Each week, the process would begin with Dobbin watching the upcoming episode on Friday. He would then collaborate closely with sound effects teams, music editors, directors, and producers to finalize the score. In spotting sessions, Dobbin worked directly with the showrunners to understand their vision for key scenes. For example, he described a memorable moment when he introduced French horns into the score to heighten the emotional intensity of a key action sequence—a decision that added a fresh dynamic while staying true to the show's rock-driven energy. These moments of collaboration were critical to the creative process, allowing Dobbin to infuse his own musical style into an already-established framework.

Dobbin emphasized how *NCIS: LA* differs from other NCIS franchises in terms of its musical style. Unlike the more traditional scores of its counterparts, *NCIS: LA* uses a modern, high-energy, and rock-infused approach to complement the show's unique tone. Over the years, Dobbin adapted the score to reflect changes in the characters and plot, evolving the music while staying true to the core identity of the series.

Beyond *NCIS: LA*, Dobbin has worked on a variety of projects, including *Shark Week*, PBS kids' shows, and documentaries. One of his upcoming projects, a psychological thriller titled *The Tasting*, has Dobbin excited to return to using a real orchestra to create a classically driven sonic experience. He shared how transitioning from TV scoring to film scoring allows for a different approach—while TV scores are often driven by tight deadlines and fast turnarounds, films offer more time for thematic development and creative exploration. This shift is refreshing for Dobbin, allowing him to push his creativity into new territories.

Dobbin's career also includes composing for commercials for brands like Samsung, Visa, McDonald's, Netflix, Marvel, and State Farm. He explained that the world of commercial composition requires a different skill set—capturing a brand's essence in mere seconds is both challenging and rewarding, especially in such a competitive space.

Throughout our conversation, Dobbin offered advice for aspiring creatives. He stressed the importance of perseverance, networking, and not being afraid of rejection. According to Dobbin, opportunities will come as long as creators stay committed to their craft and continue sharing their work with the world.

José Vieira: Viarco Pencil Co., Portugal

As the third-generation owner of Viarco Pencil Co., José Vieira offers a compelling story of how a family business can embrace creativity and collaboration to thrive in a changing world. Viarco, Portugal's only pencil manufacturer, faced major challenges following the revolution in the 1970s, when the country's shift toward democratization led to the rise of global competitors and a decline in Viarco's market share. Rather than giving up, José and his wife took a bold step in buying the company in 2011, choosing to focus on innovation and local heritage as a path forward.

Situated in São João da Madeira, an industrial town known for its labor and textile industries, Viarco benefits from its close proximity to a network of skilled artisans and cutting-edge technologies. This unique setting allows the company to blend traditional craftsmanship with modern manufacturing techniques, reimagining how a legacy business can innovate while maintaining its historical roots. José describes their factory as more than just a place of production—it's a living museum with a rich history and a platform for artistic residencies and creative experimentation.

These artistic residencies have become a hallmark of Viarco's commitment to creativity. Artists, designers, and creators from various fields are invited to work directly with Viarco's materials, exploring new possibilities for pencil design and manufacturing. These collaborations often lead to innovative products, such as specialty pencils made for artists and designers, and even customized tools for unique artistic applications. Through these partnerships, Viarco has expanded its knowledge base, drawing inspiration from a community of creative minds that challenge conventional pencil-making processes.

One of Viarco's standout innovations includes their ArtGraf line of water-soluble graphite products, designed in collaboration with artists. These products have not only redefined what a pencil can do but have also positioned Viarco as a leader in creative tools for professional artists. By encouraging this kind of experimentation, José has managed to turn a small pencil company into a hub of innovation, where traditional methods are constantly being redefined by fresh perspectives.

This blend of tradition and innovation has enabled Viarco Pencil Co. to stay relevant in a highly competitive market. By embracing creativity as a core value and fostering collaboration with the artistic community, José and his team have successfully transformed the company into a partner in artistic experimentation. Viarco is no longer just a pencil manufacturer—it's an engine for creative growth and an example of how family businesses can evolve by welcoming new ideas and maintaining connections to their heritage.

Brian Grazer: *Face to Face*

In one of my early podcast episodes, I explored *Face to Face*, a book by Oscar-winning producer Brian Grazer that dives into the transformative power of in-person encounters in fostering human connection and enhancing creativity. Drawing from his vast experience in the entertainment industry, Brian shares how face-to-face interactions have helped him overcome creative challenges and forge lasting relationships that drive innovation.

Brian believes that genuine listening—marked by openness and attentiveness—is the cornerstone of building trust and understanding. He recalls how many of his most creative breakthroughs came from meetings where he made a point to listen without distraction, allowing the other person to feel truly heard. For instance, during the development of some of his major films and television projects, including *A Beautiful Mind* and *Arrested Development*, Brian notes that face-to-face conversations often sparked new ideas or solved creative roadblocks. According to him, these interactions create a foundation of trust that allows for deeper collaboration and more authentic self-expression, which is crucial in the creative process.

In *Face to Face*, Brian also emphasizes the role of sincerity and authenticity in building relationships. He highlights Oprah Winfrey as a prime example of someone who creates powerful, lasting connections by engaging with others in an open and genuine manner. Brian advocates for embracing vulnerability, especially in moments of discomfort. He argues that while awkwardness or unease in a conversation may feel unsettling, it's often in these moments of discomfort that the most transformative connections and creative sparks emerge. Pushing through these moments, Brian asserts, allows individuals to move beyond superficial exchanges and into more meaningful dialogue.

Grazer's insights are particularly relevant to the creative industries, where collaboration and innovation thrive on authentic connections. He notes that the entertainment industry is built on relationships, and many of his projects came to life through the kind of deep, personal conversations that only happen face-to-face. Whether it was pitching a new idea, solving a problem on set, or forging partnerships, Brian's willingness to engage in real, meaningful interactions has often been the catalyst for his most successful ventures.

For readers, Brian's message is clear: be yourself in your interactions, don't shy away from vulnerability, and practice active listening in every conversation. By focusing on building trust and connection, creatives can unlock new levels of collaboration and generate ideas that might never emerge in more distant, impersonal exchanges. Brian's approach reminds us that human connection is at the heart of creativity, and embracing it can lead to profound and lasting creative breakthroughs.

***

As I reflect on the remarkable stories of collaboration from creative leaders like Vinnie Potestivo, Michael Robinson, Craig Dobbin, José Vieira, and Brian Grazer, I'm struck by the profound lessons their experiences have taught me. These individuals have shown that no matter the industry or creative discipline, it's often the relationships we build and the collaborative efforts we embrace that lead to the most transformative outcomes.

Looking back on my own career, I'm deeply grateful for the opportunities I've had to experience the power of collaboration firsthand. Whether it was through partnerships that fueled new ideas, or team efforts that carried projects through to success, the trust placed in others—sometimes even ahead of my own pursuit of excellence—became the key to lasting achievements. Collaboration isn't always easy, and it can demand vulnerability, but it has always proven to be the most rewarding part of the creative journey.

As I share my own experiences in this next section, my hope is that these reflections offer guidance for those navigating their own collaborative challenges. While striving for personal excellence is important, I've learned that trusting in the power of collaboration is even more essential in the long run. The connections we make, the trust we build, and the collective energy we harness can open doors that individual effort alone might not.

These stories are offered with the humble confidence that what I've learned along the way might help others to embrace collaboration more fully. Whether you're facing roadblocks or looking for new ways to reinvigorate your creative path, I encourage you to lean into collaboration. It's in those shared visions, the blending of strengths, and the trust we place in one another that true creative breakthroughs happen.

Moving to Hamilton Communications

In the spring of 1996, I stepped into the role of president and chief creative officer at Hamilton Communications, a move that would redefine my career and challenge the core of my creative identity. At age 36, I was navigating uncharted territory after leaving a crosstown rival, stepping into a leadership position that demanded both creative vision and collaboration.

The transition was exhilarating but daunting. From my corner office, overlooking the historic Cabrini Green housing projects, I was faced with a company full of new faces and unique challenges. Yet, this unfamiliar landscape offered a blank canvas—a chance for me to evolve as a leader and to reignite the company's creative energy through collaboration.

My first major task was improving internal and client collaboration, particularly with the Kos/DuPont partnership and AstraZeneca's new product development team. These clients were critical to our success, and building strong, synergistic relationships required recalibrating my approach. I quickly realized that leadership wasn't just about offering ideas—it was about creating a space where the team's ideas could thrive. One of the most significant challenges came during a key project for AstraZeneca, where integrating the ideas of various team members was essential to delivering a campaign that balanced innovation with the client's strategic goals.

Understanding my strengths was key to this transition. I had always thrived in the limelight, bringing energy and visibility to my creative ideas. But I soon realized that too much visibility could overshadow others, especially in collaborative settings. Creating space for the team to contribute and feel ownership over projects became an essential part of my leadership style. During a brainstorming session with the Kos/DuPont team, I found myself holding back more than usual, letting quieter voices take the lead. The results were remarkable—new perspectives emerged that I hadn't considered, and the final outcome was stronger because of it.

At the same time, I had to temper my habit of wearing my heart on my sleeve. My emotional expressiveness, while a strength, didn't always resonate with everyone. I learned to recognize when teammates preferred a quieter, more introspective environment. This shift helped me adapt my leadership style to better suit the needs of a diverse team.

One of the biggest challenges was balancing innovation with practicality. My natural inclination toward bold, off-the-wall ideas had served me well in the past, but I soon learned that those ideas needed to be grounded in feasibility. Sharing ideas more selectively and encouraging the team to balance creativity with realism became my new approach. A breakthrough moment came when we were developing a product launch campaign for AstraZeneca. While the team brainstormed unconventional ideas, I kept bringing us back to the practical constraints of the project. This balance between pushing boundaries and respecting limitations ultimately led to a successful campaign.

Optimism was another driving force behind my leadership. I've always believed that anything is possible, and this optimism often inspired the team. But I learned to ground that optimism in reality, particularly when we faced difficult challenges. It became clear that maintaining a balance between hope and pragmatism was crucial to keeping the team motivated without setting unrealistic expectations.

Finally, my passion for creativity was contagious, but I had to learn to modulate that enthusiasm for more reflective colleagues. I realized that collaboration required me to temper my excitement and listen more carefully, allowing others to contribute in their own way.

Looking back on my time at Hamilton Communications, I see it as a period of deep personal and professional growth. It was a time where collaboration became the heart of my leadership. The lessons I learned about creating space for others, balancing passion with practicality, and fostering an environment where ideas could flourish have stayed with me throughout my career. 1996 marked the start of a new era for both me and the company, as we built a culture of collaboration that laid the foundation for long-term success.

My Work with Hollister Global Branding

My work with Hollister Global Branding on market research and branding was an experience that extended far beyond analyzing data or studying trends—it was a journey that spanned borders, cultures, and professional landscapes. As a key facilitator between the sales and marketing teams, I traveled throughout Europe, engaging with nurses and leading workshops that brought together diverse team members from across the globe. This project wasn't just about gathering insights—it was about fostering collaboration across cultures to drive innovation.

From the outset, it was clear that this wasn't going to be a conventional market research project. The true challenge lay in merging the distinct perspectives of team members from different professional and cultural backgrounds. These varied viewpoints were what made the project exciting, but also what tested my collaborative skills the most.

One of the greatest lessons came from working with team members who were my opposite types—individuals who communicated or approached problems differently than I did. For example, some colleagues thrived on quick decision-making, while others preferred a more deliberate, reflective approach. This contrast in working styles forced me to recalibrate how I communicated. During a particularly intense workshop, I realized that pushing for fast solutions wasn't always the best course. Instead, I allowed for more time and space to discuss every nuance, which ultimately led to deeper, more thoughtful contributions from quieter team members. It became clear that fostering an environment where every voice had the room to contribute meaningfully would yield better results than simply driving toward a quick consensus.

Another key element of this journey was learning to respect values and principles that differed from my own. Collaboration was not just about meeting halfway—it was about understanding and valuing the unique ethos that each team member brought to the table. For instance, when working with a team of European nurses, I had to step back and truly listen to their experiences and concerns. They brought invaluable insights about patient care that fundamentally shaped how we approached the market research. It was in moments like these that I saw how personal experience deeply influenced perspectives, and I realized the importance of giving ample time for new ideas to emerge.

Patience and adaptability were essential. In one instance, a project plan had to be completely reworked due to unforeseen logistical challenges. Instead of pushing ahead with the original timeline, we took the time to reassess, adjust our approach, and give everyone involved the space to process the changes. The result? A stronger, more cohesive strategy that better reflected the needs and insights of all team members.

Ultimately, my time with Hollister Global Branding was not just about market research—it was a profound lesson in the power of cross-cultural collaboration. By respecting diverse perspectives and allowing space for different working styles, we were able to create a melody of innovation that led to successful outcomes. This experience reinforced for me the importance of effective communication and patience in achieving great results, both professionally and personally.

Insights from RELISTOR Brand at GSW

During my time at GSW, leading the strategy team for the RELISTOR brand was a journey through the complex world where medical science meets creative branding. The challenge wasn't just to understand the market for gastrointestinal disorders, but to find a way to align the precision of medical professionals with the creativity of branding, all through effective collaboration.

Collaboration became the cornerstone of our success. Working with colleagues who had deep medical and scientific expertise was invigorating but often challenging. One of the most fascinating dynamics was the difference in thinking styles, particularly when working with individuals who approached problems differently from me. Navigating these differences became an essential part of our collective journey.

A significant realization during this time was understanding the Observer personality type, which I encountered frequently. Observers are highly disciplined, meticulous, and focused on getting things exactly right. Their Introverted Thinking drives them to take their time, working through details methodically and ensuring they have the right answer before proceeding. In contrast, my approach often leaned toward decisive, bold actions, focused on moving things forward quickly. This difference in pace created friction at times, especially in high-stakes projects like RELISTOR.

For example, during a critical phase of the RELISTOR project, we were faced with a tight deadline to finalize a campaign strategy. While my instinct was to push forward and make decisions quickly, some of my colleagues—particularly those who embodied the Observer traits—preferred to dive deeper into the data before committing to a course of action. Initially, I found this slow pace frustrating, but over time, I learned to appreciate the value of their careful approach. By allowing more time for thorough analysis, we were able to uncover insights that would have otherwise been missed, leading to a more robust strategy for the brand.

Another challenge came in understanding the Observer's tendency to avoid acknowledging mistakes quickly. There was a particular moment when we were reviewing a key piece of data, and while I was ready to pivot based on new findings, some of my colleagues hesitated. They needed to double-check every detail before making any shifts. This was a lesson in patience for me—realizing that their hesitance was not about reluctance but about ensuring the decision was airtight. This meticulousness ensured that our branding and messaging for RELISTOR were not only compliant but also strategic, giving us an edge in the market.

Personal growth came from adapting my leadership style to these diverse approaches. Instead of pushing for fast decisions, I learned to give space for more thoughtful analysis. I also recognized that collaboration isn't just about aligning ideas—it's about embracing the different strengths that each team member brings. While I brought a visionary approach, the Observer's precision and caution infused our strategy with a level of depth that I could not have achieved alone.

In the world of RELISTOR, where medical accuracy and creative strategy had to coexist, learning to respect and work with the diverse thinking styles within our team was crucial. It wasn't just about mastering the market—it was about mastering the art of collaboration. By harnessing the strengths of those around me, including the Observers who brought careful analysis and deliberate thought, we were able to elevate the RELISTOR brand to new heights. This experience taught me that true collaboration isn't about changing others—it's about recognizing the value they bring and creating space for everyone to contribute their best work.

My Work with Baxter Global Oncology

Taking on the global scope of oncology market research for Baxter Global was an exhilarating journey that spanned the streets of Rome, Paris, and Berlin, along with the vibrant landscapes of Rio de Janeiro and São Paulo. As the orchestrator of focus groups with oncologists, I quickly realized that collaboration wasn't just important—it was the linchpin of success. Working with a client team that was more inclined toward analytical thinking presented both challenges and opportunities, requiring a careful balance between spontaneity and structure to achieve our goals.

Each city and country brought its own distinct perspective on the oncology landscape, but the universal truth that emerged was the need to recognize and harness the diverse strengths of every team member. My role as a facilitator meant I had to navigate different working styles, particularly with a client team that prioritized meticulous analysis. This wasn't always easy; the tendency toward data-heavy decision-making sometimes slowed down discussions, especially when I wanted to push for more dynamic, in-the-moment insights. For instance, in one session in Berlin, I found myself needing to adapt my approach when the team required more time to delve into the details, a shift from the fast-paced discussions I was used to leading.

Despite these challenges, my ability to be opportunistic and versatile became a critical asset. I treated each focus group as a living, breathing entity—an interactive performance that needed to maintain energy and momentum. My role was not just to gather data but to ensure that discussions remained lively and productive, even when navigating more analytical or structured environments. This balance of spontaneity and structure kept the sessions engaging, allowing us to extract valuable insights while respecting the analytical nature of our client's approach.

One of the key factors in our success was recognizing and leveraging my strengths as a team builder. By fostering an environment of empathy and collaboration, I helped ensure that the team's high aspirations were not only met but exceeded. My natural enthusiasm and commitment to variety infused the project with energy, keeping the team motivated across continents, whether in the more structured focus groups of Europe or the dynamic, high-energy settings in Brazil.

Cultural differences played a significant role in shaping the focus groups and team dynamics. In Rio de Janeiro, for example, the discussions were far more animated and fluid compared to the more reserved and methodical exchanges in Paris. Understanding and adapting to these cultural nuances was essential for fostering effective collaboration. I had to adjust my facilitation style to align with the local team's communication preferences, whether it was giving space for lively debates in Brazil or encouraging more structured, data-driven insights in Europe.

The outcomes of this global research were a testament to the power of collaboration. By embracing the unique attributes of each team member—whether analytical, spontaneous, or empathetic—we were able to develop a comprehensive understanding of the oncology market that transcended borders. The final insights not only met Baxter's expectations but provided a roadmap for future innovation in their oncology division. This project reinforced the idea that in global endeavors, every individual's contribution is a vital note in the harmonious composition of success.

Your Art of Collaboration

Across industries, the journeys of Vinnie Potestivo, Michael Robinson, Craig Dobbin, José Vieira, and Brian Grazer demonstrate how working together ignites creativity and drives success. Potestivo's experience at MTV showed that collective efforts could launch iconic shows like *Cribs* while adapting to the rise of interactive, social media-driven formats. In the hospitality world, Robinson applied creative thinking to enhance the guest experience, aligning innovation with financial targets and local culture to meet post-COVID demands. Dobbin, composer for *NCIS: LA*, underscored the importance of aligning with a show's vision, illustrating how persistence and teamwork can translate artistic concepts into powerful onscreen moments. Meanwhile, Vieira revitalized his family's Viarco Pencil Co. by merging local craftsmanship with modern technology, using artist residencies and partnerships to maintain tradition and spur new ideas. Finally, Grazer highlighted the power of in-person connections, explaining how genuine listening and openness can foster transformative collaborations.

From media to hospitality, music to manufacturing, each story shows that bringing diverse voices together unlocks innovation that far surpasses what any single contributor can achieve alone. These stories reveal how collaboration, whether in media, hospitality, music, or family businesses, leads to creative breakthroughs that exceed what can be achieved alone. By integrating diverse voices and skill sets, the power of collaboration fosters innovation across every field.

Reflecting on my own experiences, the RELISTOR brand project, Baxter Global Oncology, and my work with Hollister Global Branding stand as testaments to the transformative power of collaboration. Each of these case studies revealed that success was built not just on individual expertise, but on the synergy of diverse perspectives working toward a common goal. From navigating cultural nuances to balancing analytical and creative thinking, collaboration was the key to creating strategies that resonated globally.

In conclusion, collaboration is an essential component of creative success. It's about harnessing the power of collective ideas, building connections, and creating an environment where each voice contributes to the whole. By embracing collaboration, you not only unlock new perspectives and opportunities, but also set the stage for growth in both your creative work and professional journey. Whether you're just starting out or looking to reinvigorate your creativity, the art of collaboration will propel you toward new heights of innovation.

Key Takeaways

- Collaboration accelerates artistic growth by blending diverse ideas and skills.

- In-person connections and genuine listening are essential for fostering trust and creativity.

- Aligning creativity with business goals ensures sustainable success.

- Embracing cultural and working style differences enriches collaborative efforts, leading to more robust outcomes.

Questions

1. Learning from Vinnie Potestivo's MTV Journey: How can the evolution of traditional television formats to interactive and personal content influence your creative storytelling? In what ways can you leverage awards and personal branding to enhance your creative visibility and impact?

2. Applying Michael Robinson's Hospitality Insights: In what ways can you incorporate local and cultural elements into your creative work to enhance audience engagement?

3. How can you adapt your creative voice to align with the vision of collaborators, as exemplified by Craig Dobbin in TV and film music composition?

4.   How can challenges in a family business, as faced by José Vieira, be transformed into opportunities for innovation and sustained growth?

5.   In what ways can in-person encounters, inspired by Brian Grazer's philosophy, enhance your collaborative efforts and creativity?

6.   How might understanding and navigating diverse thinking styles, as explored in my GSW-RELISTOR case study, contribute to more effective collaboration in your field?

7.   In the context of the Baxter Global Oncology Market Research case study, how can recognizing and leveraging diverse strengths enhance collaboration in your team?

LESSON FOUR

Mastering the Numbers of Your Business

One key to creative success lies in understanding how to balance artistic ambition with business strategy. By mastering the financial aspects of your craft, you can ensure sustainability, innovation, and growth, turning your passion into a thriving enterprise. In this lesson, we explore the importance of treating creativity as a business—understanding the financial principles that support long-term success. In creative work, passion and artistry often take priority, but financial management is just as critical for long-term success. After speaking with 250 creatives worldwide, I found that viewing creativity as a business is necessary to maintain and grow your work. Understanding the numbers—things like profit and loss, cash flow, and budgeting—is a vital part of sustaining creative endeavors.

This lesson will explain how to use these financial tools to make better decisions, manage projects, and create new opportunities. Managing creativity as a business isn't just about being financially responsible—it's about making your creative work more efficient, scalable, and sustainable.

We will look at examples from Dorothy Kolb, Tim Tortora, Joanne Butcher, Bree Noble, and Tames Rietjek—creatives who have successfully brought business skills into their work. Their stories show how proper financial management leads to greater artistic control, improved decision-making, and financial stability over time.

I'll also share personal lessons, including times when a lack of understanding about financial data affected the outcome of certain projects. By reflecting on these experiences, I hope to show how learning to manage The Numbers can make a tangible difference in the success of creative projects.

Approaching your creative work with a business mindset adds financial value and ensures its long-term sustainability. Mastering The Numbers equips you to make more informed choices, expand your opportunities, and keep your creative projects thriving.

Dorothy Kolb: DK East Associates

Dorothy Kolb, an expert in media finance and operations, emphasizes the importance of managing creativity with a strong financial foundation. With her background at CBS Sports, Fox Sports, and NBC, she brings deep experience in navigating the intersection of creativity and finance. Now at the helm of DK East Associates, Dorothy works closely with creatives to ensure they understand the financial side of their businesses, a critical element often neglected in favor of passion-driven projects.

She recognizes the common challenge that many creatives face— neglecting their own financial well-being while focusing on making an impact or sharing their artistic vision. Dorothy stresses the importance of understanding profit and loss, budgeting, and cash flow to maintain a balanced approach that supports both creativity and business sustainability. She helps clients assess their pricing strategies, manage their cash flow, and understand how to measure the profitability of their projects.

Dorothy's role extends beyond simply providing financial services. She acts as an educator, showing entrepreneurs how knowing their numbers empowers them to make better business decisions. She advocates for creatives to outsource financial tasks if needed, reassuring them that seeking help is a strength, not a weakness. Her upcoming online course aims to teach financial literacy in an accessible way, breaking down complex concepts into actionable steps for creatives to implement.

Since the pandemic, Dorothy has noticed a shift in how her clients view spending. Many are moving away from the traditional "spend more to make more" mindset, opting instead for cost-effective strategies that maintain quality while reducing waste. This has led to more sustainable practices, with creatives reassessing their budgets and finding ways to do more with less. Dorothy's guidance in this area has helped many of her clients adjust to these new economic realities without compromising on the quality of their work.

One of Dorothy's key messages to creatives is to understand their worth. She encourages them to communicate their value confidently and recognize that they are offering more than just a service based on an hourly rate. Dorothy's journey from a successful corporate career to becoming an entrepreneur and a financial advocate for creatives serves as a powerful reminder of the importance of combining creativity with financial responsibility.

Through her work, Dorothy Kolb is a thought leader in helping creatives manage their businesses effectively, ensuring that their passion projects are not only financially viable but positioned for long-term success.

Tim Tortura: *Hollywood Accounting*

Tim Tortura, a Hollywood CFO and veteran movie producer, emphasizes the need for creatives to view themselves as business professionals, especially in the entertainment industry. With over 35 years of experience, Tim teaches artists the importance of mastering profit and loss in their work. His key message is that filmmakers and creatives must treat themselves as CEOs of their own businesses, constantly working on selling, networking, and taking ownership of their financial health.

Tim outlines two primary paths for filmmakers: working with corporate studios or pursuing independent opportunities through film festivals, competitions, and showcases. He highlights the importance of understanding industry trends, crafting an effective pitch, and maintaining a high level of professionalism. For independent filmmakers, he stresses the need to build relationships with key players in the industry—financiers, production companies, and distributors. These connections are essential for getting a project off the ground, whether it's through a large studio or an independent production.

One of the biggest challenges, Tim explains, is that creatives are often the last to get paid. Understanding the financial structure of filmmaking is critical, from budgeting and contracts to residuals and managing production costs. Tim dives into the specifics of how financiers and production companies control the flow of money, and how creatives can protect themselves by negotiating smart contracts and ensuring transparent accounting practices.

Drawing from his book, *Hollywood Accounting*, Tim shares personal stories of being cheated by the system, offering lessons learned from decades of navigating the industry. His book uncovers the pitfalls many creatives face, such as hidden fees and unclear accounting, and offers practical solutions for avoiding these traps. Tim's guidance encourages filmmakers to take control of their financial literacy, ensuring they understand the flow of money from production to distribution, so they can make more informed decisions and avoid being taken advantage of.

For independent filmmakers, Tim advises on specific steps to showcase their work, such as building a strategic online presence, submitting to the right festivals, and developing a strong network of contacts. By understanding the business side of filmmaking and actively managing finances, creatives can secure their financial future while continuing to pursue their artistic vision.

Joanne Butcher: Filmmakers Success

Joanne Butcher, an expert in film financing and screenwriting, underscores the importance of financial management for independent filmmakers. With her extensive experience, Joanne guides filmmakers through the often complicated processes of funding, production, and distribution. One of her key messages is the need to debunk the myth that simply getting into a film festival guarantees distribution. Instead, she stresses that filmmakers must understand the business side of their craft from the very beginning.

Joanne teaches filmmakers to align their creative vision with a solid financial strategy. She encourages them to begin every project by thinking about the end goal—how the film will generate revenue, attract investors, and ultimately reach its audience. This approach requires filmmakers to take an active role in planning for the financial future of their project, rather than leaving it up to chance. Budgeting, understanding the costs of production, and knowing how to pitch to investors are central to her guidance.

Joanne helps filmmakers connect with potential investors, focusing on building relationships early in the process. She teaches creatives how to present their projects as financially viable ventures, emphasizing the importance of clear communication around expected returns and associated risks. In addition to working with filmmakers, Joanne also educates investors on the unique dynamics of the film industry. By helping investors understand both the risks and potential rewards of film investments, Joanne bridges the gap between the creative and financial worlds. This education benefits filmmakers by making it easier for them to secure funding and build confidence in their business acumen.

One example of Joanne's impact involves an independent filmmaker she coached through the process of securing investors for a documentary. By following her advice—crafting a strong pitch, managing production costs effectively, and building a distribution plan—this filmmaker not only completed the project but also secured a distribution deal that exceeded expectations. This success story illustrates how Joanne's approach gives filmmakers the tools they need to navigate the complexities of the industry while maintaining their creative vision.

For aspiring filmmakers, Joanne's insights provide a roadmap for combining artistic ambition with financial success. By emphasizing the need for financial literacy, Joanne helps creatives manage their projects with a business-minded approach, ensuring that their films are not only completed but also positioned for long-term success.

Bree Noble: Female Musician Academy

Bree Noble is dedicated to helping musicians transition from being creative talents to running their music careers as businesses. Through her work as CEO of the Female Musician Academy, Bree provides guidance on the financial management and strategic thinking required to build a successful career in the music industry. She emphasizes that musicians need to treat their careers as businesses, developing the financial acumen necessary to support long-term growth.

Bree highlights the importance of going beyond raw talent, explaining that taking risks and persevering through setbacks is essential. She dispels the myth that success in the music industry is purely a result of luck or going viral, instead stressing the importance of hard work and a deliberate approach to career-building. Her teachings focus on the need for musicians to develop a range of skills, from marketing and networking to financial planning.

Her own journey began with a focus on supporting female musicians, but Bree has since expanded her work to assist artists of all genders in creating multiple income streams from their music. Independent musicians often have to wear multiple hats—managing their own finances, promotions, and career development—and Bree equips them with the tools to succeed in these areas. She emphasizes the need for musicians to approach their careers with a business mindset, using a combination of strategic planning and financial discipline to achieve their goals.

Bree draws clear parallels between building a music career and starting a small business, pointing out the importance of networking, referrals, and slowly growing a fan base. She challenges the belief that success is tied to being in a major music city, explaining how digital platforms like YouTube, Spotify, and Patreon allow musicians to connect with a global audience from anywhere.

Bree also outlines various ways musicians can generate income, including freelancing, session work, teaching, and creating exclusive fan content. She highlights real-life examples of artists using platforms like Patreon to offer exclusive access to their music, merchandise, and performances, all while building loyal communities of fans. Bree teaches musicians to focus on developing deep connections with their audience to monetize their music sustainably.

In her creative process, Bree addresses the challenge of facing a blank page by using deadlines to push through and deliver raw content, allowing ideas to flow naturally. She also stresses the importance of mentorship and community support. Bree encourages female musicians to connect with other creatives, learn from their experiences, and build supportive networks, especially through online communities and platforms.

Bree Noble's interview underscores the changing landscape of the music industry, where financial literacy and strategic planning are essential for success. She also emphasizes the value of mentorship and community-building, particularly for female musicians, as they navigate the complexities of turning their passion into a sustainable career.

Tames Rietjek:
Director at The Ocean Cleanup

Tames Rietjek, a highly accomplished C-level executive, transitioned from a career in financial markets, sustainability performance, and business data science to a leadership role at The Ocean Cleanup in Rotterdam, Netherlands. With a proven track record in financial crime prevention and stakeholder management, Tames now focuses on leading efforts to rid the world's oceans of plastic pollution.

At The Ocean Cleanup, Tames applies his expertise in data analysis and strategic planning to tackle one of the most pressing environmental challenges: plastic pollution in rivers. According to Tames, only about 1,000 rivers—out of the 30,000 to 35,000 rivers globally—are responsible for the vast majority (80% to 85%) of plastic waste that enters the oceans. These rivers are primarily located in Southeast Asia, Central, and South America. By focusing on these specific rivers, the organization can target efforts where they are most needed.

Tames and his team have deployed advanced river technology solutions designed to capture plastic and other waste before it reaches the ocean. These systems act as barriers, preventing trash from entering open waters and allowing for its safe removal. Tames emphasizes that the goal is twofold: to remove legacy plastic already in the ocean and to stop the flow of new pollution by "closing the tap." This focus on numbers and data-driven strategies has allowed The Ocean Cleanup to maximize its impact and ensure resources are used effectively.

Under Tames' leadership, The Ocean Cleanup has seen measurable success in its efforts to reduce plastic pollution. For example, the deployment of these river systems has already made significant strides in reducing waste in high-pollution areas, contributing to long-term environmental restoration. Tames' ability to apply business insights and financial strategy to sustainability challenges demonstrates how focusing on the numbers can create meaningful, lasting change in the world.

***

As we've seen from the stories of Dorothy Kolb, Tim Tortura, Joanne Butcher, Bree Noble, and Tames Rietjek, the most successful creatives understand that the key to long-term sustainability lies in approaching their work with a business mindset. Whether in filmmaking, music, or environmental activism, embracing financial literacy, strategic thinking, and the power of numbers is essential to transforming passion into a lasting career. These individuals have demonstrated how mastering the financial aspects of their industries not only supports their creative endeavors but also elevates their work to new levels of impact and success.

Throughout my own journey, I've learned similar lessons. Like many creatives, I initially focused more on the artistic side of my work, believing that talent and dedication alone were enough to reach my goals. But as my career progressed, I discovered that understanding the financial and strategic dimensions of creativity was equally important. Knowing how to balance budgets, manage resources, and align creative efforts with business objectives made the difference between simply completing a project and achieving something truly impactful.

Next, I'll share my personal experiences of integrating a business mindset into my creative work. From navigating complex client relationships to managing large-scale campaigns, I'll reflect on how financial management, strategic planning, and a focus on numbers have shaped my approach. These experiences taught me that creativity and business are not separate pursuits but are, in fact, deeply connected—each enhancing and supporting the other.

Approaching creative work as a business doesn't just safeguard its sustainability; it also amplifies its potential. By treating creativity as an enterprise, we ensure that our artistic passions have the foundation they need to thrive and grow in an ever-evolving landscape.

My Proposal to Merck KGaA

In the field of pharmaceutical sales training, my work with Merck KGaA began with a series of successful workshops across the Asia-Pacific region. Over three years, we built a strong rapport with their sales teams, delivering programs that were tailored to the specific needs of this diverse and dynamic market. Then came an exciting challenge: Merck KGaA's leadership approached us with a proposal to create a global sales training curriculum—an ambitious leap that would extend far beyond our regional efforts.

At first, the idea of taking our proven success on a global scale was invigorating, but as we began to build the proposal, the numbers told a different story. The initial budget projections showed that our vision for a worldwide program was not feasible within the company's financial constraints. We quickly realized that to move forward, we needed to strike a balance between creative ambition and financial reality.

When I presented the proposal to Merck KGaA's decision-makers, I knew that our ability to manage expectations was key. Instead of pushing for an all-or-nothing global expansion, we focused on addressing their immediate needs—the areas where we could add value right away—while outlining a scalable plan for future growth. This allowed us to offer a step-by-step approach that could be expanded over time, without overwhelming their budget or resources.

Transparency played a crucial role in building trust. We were clear about both the opportunities and the challenges of creating a global curriculum, ensuring that Merck KGaA's leadership had a realistic understanding of what could be achieved. We used data from our Asia-Pacific success, along with case studies and measurable outcomes, to show the potential impact of our approach, but we were careful not to overpromise.

In the end, although the full global initiative couldn't be implemented immediately, our honest approach laid the foundation for a strong, long-term partnership. By acknowledging the financial constraints and offering a sustainable path forward, we established ourselves as trusted partners who understood the importance of balancing vision with pragmatism.

This experience underscored the importance of incorporating financial discipline into creative proposals. While our original idea had to be scaled back, our attention to the numbers helped us craft a plan that was both ambitious and achievable, ensuring that Merck KGaA could see the value in working with us for years to come.

Expanding My Mind for an Abbott/Reata Account Launch

In the competitive field of market research and account planning, the pitch for the Abbott/Reata account launch stood as a prime example of combining strategic innovation with financial insight. Our goal was not only to secure a new business partnership but also to extend its reach on a global scale—a challenge that required a creative, yet practical, approach.

I proposed a plan that aligned new business market research with existing travel schedules in key cities, including Rome, Paris, Berlin, and Dallas. By leveraging these international travel plans, we were able to streamline logistical complexities and conduct market research across diverse regions in a cost-effective manner. This approach provided the client with global insights while minimizing additional expenses, making the project more financially viable.

A major component of this pitch's success lay in the financial planning that accompanied it. We ensured that the numbers aligned with the client's expectations, presenting a clear plan that balanced both immediate needs and long-term scalability. This attention to financial feasibility demonstrated our ability to manage resources efficiently, while still delivering high-impact results.

Our pitch wasn't just about addressing current needs—it was about looking toward the future. By envisioning growth opportunities for the client, we introduced an optimistic yet realistic strategy that showcased our resourcefulness. We weren't afraid to push boundaries, embracing creative solutions in account planning that set us apart from more conventional approaches.

In particular, our focus on innovative strategies made this pitch stand out. By introducing imaginative ideas in market research and lead generation, we positioned ourselves as forward-thinking partners who could identify high-value opportunities. This approach demonstrated that we were not only capable of delivering results but also of continuously driving innovation in the client's business.

The Abbott/Reata account launch pitch reflected a careful balance of strategic thinking, financial discipline, and creative problem-solving. It positioned us as visionary partners capable of delivering on global aspirations while remaining grounded in financial realities. Our blend of responsiveness, intuition, and resourcefulness ultimately secured the account and set the stage for a successful partnership.

My overall business and selling style combines financial acumen, personal connection, and contagious energy. I keep a close eye on the P&L aspects of creative business, ensuring that we meet financial targets while building strong relationships with clients. By moving fluidly between business discussions and personal interactions, I foster a sense of relatability and trust that strengthens these connections.

While I excel in building relationships, I recognize the importance of focusing more on follow-up and implementation. I've developed strategies to ensure that promising relationships are followed through with strong execution, helping to translate opportunities into tangible outcomes. My adaptability and leadership are key assets, allowing me to guide both colleagues and clients toward successful outcomes in a fast-paced environment.

My selling style merges interpersonal skills, energetic networking, and a clear understanding of the financial intricacies that underpin successful creative projects. By combining these elements, I ensure that every interaction—whether with clients or internal teams—leads to strategic, results-driven partnerships.

The Numbers:
Managing Your Creativity as a Business

Success in the creative world requires more than just artistic talent—it demands a firm grasp of the financial elements that support and grow creative ventures. In this chapter, we've explored the entrepreneurial side of creativity, focusing on how mastering financial management and treating creativity as a business leads to long-term sustainability. The experiences of Dorothy Kolb, Tim Tortora, Joanne Butcher, Bree Noble, and Tames Rietjek provide valuable lessons on integrating business acumen into creative work.

- Dorothy Kolb stresses the importance of balancing passion with financial discipline. She encourages creatives to embrace outsourcing where necessary, ensuring that they have the support to manage their finances effectively while focusing on their strengths.

- Tim Tortora views artists as CEOs of their own businesses. He highlights the importance of selling, networking, and keeping up with industry trends. Whether working with major studios or pursuing independent paths, artists must approach their careers with a business mindset to succeed.

- Joanne Butcher emphasizes aligning creative vision with a strong financial plan. She dispels myths about automatic success through film festivals, urging filmmakers to have a clear understanding of the business side of their craft from the start, ensuring they plan for revenue and distribution.

- Bree Noble demonstrates how musicians can turn their talent into a sustainable career by thinking like small business owners. She stresses the importance of taking risks, building a loyal fanbase, and developing multiple revenue streams to ensure long-term success.

- Tames Rietjek transitioned from financial markets to leading The Ocean Cleanup, where he applies data-driven strategies to address environmental challenges. By using numbers and analytics, Tames and his team are effectively tackling global issues like plastic pollution in rivers, showing how financial strategy can fuel innovation.

- My experiences with Merck KGaA and Abbott/Reata reinforced the importance of balancing ambition with realistic financial planning. With Merck KGaA, I focused on transparency and scaling responsibly, while with Abbott/Reata, I employed creative strategies and built visionary partnerships that combined personal connection with financial discipline.

Tapping into these stories, we've uncovered the critical role of financial acumen in creative work. Managing creativity as a business isn't just about expressing passion; it's about ensuring sustainability, driving innovation, and finding the right balance between artistic ambition and profitability. By applying the lessons learned from these professionals—and from my own journey—creatives can harness the power of numbers to sustain and grow their work, turning their talents into lasting, successful ventures.

Questions

1. Reflecting on Dorothy Kolb's insights, how can you strike a balance between your passion-driven creativity and sound financial practices in your creative endeavors?

2. In Tim Tortora's case study, how might you adopt the mindset of treating yourself as a CEO in your creative pursuits? What steps can you take to constantly sell and network, aligning with his entrepreneurial approach?

3. Joanne Butcher emphasizes the importance of aligning creative vision with financial strategy. How can you apply this principle to your own creative projects, ensuring attention to both the artistic and financial aspects?

4. Drawing from Bree Noble's interview, how can musicians transition from viewing their creative talents as a passion to establishing a music career as a viable business proposition? What risks and perseverance strategies resonate with your own creative journey?

5. Considering Dorothy's call to action about knowing your value, how confident are you in communicating your worth in your creative pursuits? What steps can you take to enhance your confidence and recognition of your value beyond just an hourly rate?

6. In Tim's discussion of the film industry, what industry trends, pitching strategies, and professional behaviors can you incorporate into your creative process, especially if your work involves collaboration with others or seeks financial backing?

7. Bree Noble emphasizes the importance of community and mentorship for women entrepreneurs in the music industry. How can you actively seek out and contribute to a supportive community in your creative field? What role can mentorship play in your professional development?

8. How cautious are you about making promises that you may not be able to deliver? What steps do you take to maintain the integrity of your commitments while aiming to exceed expectations?

9. How comfortable are you in responding to requests for financial assistance? In what ways do you balance task-oriented objectives with financial considerations in your account planning?

LESSON FIVE

Anticipating Obstacles in Your Creative Process

The creative process is full of unexpected challenges, and the ability to overcome them is essential for long-term success. In this lesson, we focus on the importance of having contingency plans—strategic solutions that turn potential obstacles into manageable steps forward. Being adaptable and prepared for obstacles can transform challenges into opportunities. By anticipating potential setbacks, creatives can navigate through unexpected changes with resilience and strategic foresight.

Through interviews with Allyson Hernandez, Rebecca King Crews, and Valerie Leonard, we'll see how successful creatives anticipate challenges and develop plans that allow them to adapt and thrive. Allyson Hernandez embodies resilience and adaptability, as shown through her creative journey in writing *Ballad of Dreams*. She highlights the importance of being able to reinvent oneself at any stage in life. Rebecca King Crews showcases the balance between authenticity and family in her career. She underscores the power of staying true to oneself and making decisions that reflect one's personal values, even in the face of industry pressure. Valerie Leonard focuses on values, ethics, and the importance of succession planning in the non-profit world. Her approach helps organizations ensure leadership stability and maintain momentum despite leadership transitions or unforeseen challenges. This proactive approach isn't just about avoiding risks; it's about staying resilient when things don't go as expected.

I will also share personal examples where having—or lacking—a backup plan made a significant difference. In my own experience with the Solstice MYOBLOC account, I learned the hard lesson of failing to account for team dynamics and how not having a contingency plan contributed to losing the account. This taught me to appreciate the importance of strategic planning, team coordination, and adapting quickly when client expectations change.

These stories illustrate the value of preparing ahead, allowing creatives to handle setbacks with confidence and turn challenges into opportunities. Contingency planning is more than just reacting to problems; it's a practical way to stay adaptable and ensure success, even when the unexpected happens. By planning for potential obstacles, creatives can navigate challenges with confidence and maintain progress on their journey toward sustained success.

Allyson Hernandez: 'Ballad of Dreams'

Allyson Hernandez is a multi-talented creative who exemplifies resilience and the ability to adapt in pursuit of her dreams. With experience in executive coaching, acting, composing, and entrepreneurship, Allyson's story highlights the importance of contingency planning and the power of pivoting when faced with challenges.

Her book, *Ballad of Dreams*, reflects her belief in flexibility. The story, set in the worlds of musical theater and historical fiction, explores themes of friendship and self-discovery. Through characters like Audrey and Rose, Allyson touches on the pursuit of independence and how important it is to adapt to life's changes. These themes mirror her own journey, which has been marked by diverse roles and an openness to change.

Allyson embraces the diversity of her pursuits—as a Certified Executive Coach, a musician, and an entrepreneur—and sees this variety as a source of strength. She believes that creatives shouldn't feel pressured to conform or "blend in," but should instead celebrate their individuality. Her story is a testament to self-expression and empowerment, particularly for women pursuing their dreams.

One of Allyson's key strengths is her ability to reinvent herself at different stages of life. She has shifted from corporate HR to the world of creative coaching and writing, proving that creative aspirations aren't confined by age or a set timeline. Her journey shows that adapting to new opportunities is a crucial part of creative growth.

When I spoke with Allyson again two years later, her creative journey had continued to evolve. From the book, her work expanded into a soundtrack album and a Broadway company reading, illustrating her belief that dreams continue to grow and change over time.

Allyson also understands the importance of feedback in the creative process. She emphasizes the need to filter feedback wisely, so that it fosters growth without diluting the original vision. This balance—between staying true to your art and being open to criticism—is essential, and Allyson's approach provides a guide for managing this aspect of the journey.

A core part of her philosophy is contingency planning. She recognizes that both life and creative work are unpredictable, and having a backup plan ensures that challenges don't derail progress. Her ability to blend varied interests and roles demonstrates that adaptability is a strength, not a compromise.

As Allyson says, "Life is like that. The big, bold colors can live in harmony with the gray, and it's beautiful to me." Through her story, Allyson encourages creatives to embrace both the vibrant and subtle aspects of their journey, finding beauty in every shade and creating a path that is uniquely their own.

Rebecca King Crews: R&B Singer Balancing Fame with Family

Rebecca King Crews is an artist who has successfully balanced her roles as a singer, songwriter, and actress with her responsibilities as a mother and wife. Known for her work in adult contemporary and R&B music, she has chosen to prioritize her family throughout her career while still pursuing her passion for music.

In 2018, Rebecca made a bold decision to release music under the pseudonym "Regina Madre." Her goal was to step out of the public eye and receive feedback on her music without the influence of her name or public persona. The singles "(I Keep) Holding On" and "Destiny" were well-received, gaining attention on the radio. However, she soon realized that performing under a pseudonym didn't provide the authentic connection with her audience that she desired. Rebecca decided to return to her real name, finding that transparency and a genuine relationship with her fans were more important than staying anonymous.

While navigating the complexities of the music industry, Rebecca has consistently put family at the forefront of her decisions. At various points in her career, she took breaks from performing to focus on her family, showing an unwavering commitment to supporting her loved ones. Despite stepping out of the spotlight at times, Rebecca has continued to write and develop new music, finding ways to balance her creative drive with her personal values.

Rebecca's journey is a powerful example of how staying true to oneself and maintaining a focus on what matters most can lead to a fulfilling life. Her decision to put family first, even in the face of a demanding career, demonstrates her commitment to creating a meaningful legacy that goes beyond the stage. As she continues to write and perform, Rebecca serves as an inspiration to others who seek to balance their professional ambitions with their personal lives.

Valerie Leonard, NonProfit Utopia

Valerie Leonard is dedicated to empowering non-profit organizations and communities to thrive through strategic guidance and leadership development. With a focus on cultivating values and ethics, Valerie aims to create a more equitable non-profit sector, ensuring that organizations are equipped to serve their communities effectively.

One of Valerie's core missions is to support grassroots organizations, working closely with local communities to ensure they have the resources and knowledge needed to make a meaningful impact. She emphasizes the importance of community involvement, believing that change comes from within the community itself. Through her guidance, these organizations are able to enhance their strategic planning and strengthen their leadership structures.

A key component of Valerie's work is helping non-profits navigate the often-challenging grant proposal process. She provides training on how to identify potential funding sources, craft compelling proposals, and build relationships with funders. Valerie's expertise helps organizations secure the necessary financial support to continue their work and expand their reach.

In addition to securing funding, Valerie highlights the critical role of succession planning in maintaining organizational momentum. She teaches non-profits how to develop strong leadership pipelines and prepare for transitions, ensuring that the organization remains stable and effective even when key leaders move on. Her approach includes developing clear succession strategies and training the next generation of leaders to step confidently into their roles.

Valerie's commitment to ethical leadership and her passion for creating sustainable organizations have made her a respected figure in the non-profit world. Through her leadership programs and training initiatives, she is actively shaping the future of non-profits by fostering the development of emerging leaders who are equipped to tackle the challenges of tomorrow.

***

As I reflect on the stories shared by Allyson Hernandez, Rebecca King Crews, and Valerie Leonard, I am reminded of the resilience and adaptability that define the creative journey. These individuals have faced unexpected challenges and navigated through them with grace, foresight, and a deep commitment to their values. Their stories serve as powerful reminders that preparation and anticipation of obstacles are not just necessary but instrumental in fostering long-term growth and success.

In the creative world, challenges are inevitable. Whether it's balancing personal and professional responsibilities like Rebecca, fostering leadership and strategic thinking like Valerie, or pivoting in response to unexpected turns like Allyson, growth comes not just from overcoming obstacles but from preparing for them.

As I transition to sharing my own experiences, I do so with a sense of gratitude for the lessons learned along the way. The moments of uncertainty and challenge, which could have easily derailed progress, became opportunities for reflection, adaptation, and ultimately, growth. It's through preparation—whether through contingency plans or strategic foresight—that I've been able to navigate these hurdles and continue moving forward.

Now, looking into my own journey, I hope to offer insights that might help you in your creative path—reminding us all that preparing for obstacles is not just about avoiding failure, but about building resilience and turning setbacks into stepping stones toward greater success.

My Failure to See the Impact of Team Change with Solstice/MYOBLOC

In the unpredictable world of agency-client relationships, I encountered a pivotal challenge when the Solstice MYOBLOC account announced they were putting our agency up for review. This unexpected development highlighted a key lesson in contingency planning and the need to adapt quickly to unforeseen changes.

I had invested significant creative energy and personal dedication into the project, believing that our strong creative work would solidify our relationship with the client. However, a major team change within the client's organization shifted their priorities—something I didn't fully grasp at the time. While I remained focused on delivering bold ideas, the client had begun seeking more stability, reliability, and a sense of continuity that I hadn't addressed.

This failure to recognize the impact of the team change was a wake-up call. As client expectations shifted, I realized that creativity alone wouldn't suffice. The situation required a deeper understanding of how internal dynamics affected the client's perception of our agency. I needed to bring organizational skills, time management, and a proactive strategy to the forefront—qualities that weren't naturally part of my creative process but were critical to maintaining client trust.

Looking back, I can see that my tendency to rely on spontaneous creativity and avoid structured planning had contributed to the loss of the account. I also realized the importance of valuing diverse perspectives within the team. I had favored working with those who shared my creative mindset, but in moments of crisis, it became clear that a diverse team—one that could offer a range of problem-solving approaches—was essential for success.

We ultimately lost the Solstice MYOBLOC account, and it was a hard lesson. However, it also marked a turning point in how I approached future client relationships. I began to place a greater emphasis on contingency planning, ensuring that every project had a strategic roadmap that balanced creative freedom with client needs. I became more intentional about anticipating challenges and adapting quickly when client expectations shifted.

The experience underscored the reality that while creativity is a powerful asset, it must be supported by planning, organization, and a readiness to pivot when the unexpected occurs. This failure became the foundation for future success, shaping how I approached new accounts with a stronger focus on adaptability and client trust.

How to Prepare for Obstacles with Contingency Planning

In this lesson, we've discussed how flexibility and adaptation are crucial when facing creative challenges. Contingency planning is the key to being prepared for obstacles and ensuring that unexpected issues don't derail progress:

- Allyson Hernandez demonstrates how resilience allows for continuous growth. Her ability to reinvent herself, as shown in her creative journey with Ballad of Dreams, highlights the importance of staying adaptable at every stage of life.

- Rebecca King Crews shows the power of authenticity and maintaining a balance between family and career. By choosing to stay true to herself, she found more meaningful connections with her audience.

- Valerie Leonard highlights the value of ethics and succession planning in non-profit organizations. She emphasizes how leaders can prepare for change by developing strong strategies and leadership pipelines to ensure sustainability.

- My experience with the Solstice MYOBLOC account reinforced the importance of having a contingency plan. The unpredictable nature of agency-client relationships taught me to focus on strategic planning, appreciate the contributions of all team members, and remain adaptable to changes in team dynamics and client needs.

The ability to prepare for the unexpected allows you to respond quickly when challenges arise, turning potential setbacks into opportunities for growth. Contingency planning is a vital tool for navigating the uncertainties of creative work and ensuring long-term success.

As you move forward, embrace strategic foresight as part of your creative process. By anticipating challenges and being prepared with backup plans, you'll be better equipped to navigate obstacles and thrive in the ever-changing landscape of creativity. Ultimately, preparing for obstacles, through the development of contingency plans, empowers creatives to thrive in uncertain environments and turn potential setbacks into stepping stones toward success.

Key Takeaways

- Contingency planning allows creatives to anticipate challenges and ensure their projects stay on track, even in unpredictable situations.

- Flexibility and adaptability are essential qualities for transforming setbacks into growth opportunities.

- Recognizing the importance of strategic foresight ensures that creatives can navigate obstacles while maintaining trust, stability, and progress in their work.

Questions

1. How does Allyson Hernandez's diverse background in executive coaching, acting, composing, and entrepreneurship exemplify the versatility of creativity? How can you apply a multi-faceted approach to your creative endeavors?

2. In Allyson's emphasis on breaking free from societal norms and celebrating individuality, how can you infuse your unique personality and perspectives into your creative work? Reflect on instances where societal expectations may have influenced your creativity.

3. Considering Valerie Leonard's commitment to guiding non-profit leaders and organizations, how can a focus on values and ethics enhance the impact of creative initiatives? Explore ways to integrate values into your creative projects for a meaningful outcome.

4. Rebecca King Crews chose to prioritize family over fame. How does her decision resonate with the idea of finding a harmonious balance between personal and professional life in creative pursuits? Reflect on instances where you can strike a better balance in your creative journey.

5. Allyson's insights on filtering feedback for artistic growth highlight the delicate balance between staying true to one's vision and being open to constructive criticism. How can you cultivate a mindset that welcomes feedback as a catalyst for improvement while maintaining your artistic integrity?

6. Drawing from the agency-client relationship case study, reflect on a time when unforeseen challenges disrupted your creative plans. How can you integrate contingency

planning into your creative process to navigate unexpected obstacles effectively?

7. In the Solstice MYOBLOC account case, the failure to see the impact of a team change led to challenges. How can you enhance your awareness of team dynamics in your creative collaborations? Consider instances where understanding team dynamics could have improved your creative outcomes.

LESSON SIX

Developing Your Creative Leadership Influence

Leadership is a crucial aspect of the creative process, shaping the path to success and guiding individuals toward achieving their goals, focusing on how visionaries can inspire and guide others toward innovation and success.

This lesson explores the stories of mentors and leaders who have played pivotal roles in the lives of successful creatives, including Janet Attwood, creator of "The Passion Test," Dr. Bill Dorfman, known for his work on *Extreme Makeover* and founding the LEAP Foundation, Jonathan Knight, who transitioned from game creator to head of games at *The New York Times*, and YaYa Zazueta, a driving force in her community.

Attwood is a catalyst for personal and creative transformation through "The Passion Test," a tool that helps individuals unlock their purpose. Her approach, rooted in self-awareness and gratitude, teaches creatives to overcome self-limiting beliefs and embrace their potential. Dorfman, known as the "dentist to the stars," exemplifies how leadership and creativity intersect in the world of cosmetic dentistry. His work with the LEAP Foundation shows his commitment to mentoring the next generation of leaders, emphasizing skills like communication and networking. Knight, Head of NYT Games, highlights the strategic importance of creativity in business. He illustrates how games can drive customer engagement and retention, offering a model for blending creativity with business strategy. And, Zazueta, through Alma de Pueblo, demonstrates how creativity can serve a community by preserving traditions and creating a platform for social change. Her work emphasizes the role of leadership in championing both culture and commerce. Their examples offer concrete lessons on how to embrace leadership roles and navigate creative challenges effectively.

These individuals represent the power of leadership to spark creativity and inspiration in others. Through their leadership styles and approaches, they have helped reshape industries, mentor new talent, and elevate creative work to new heights. Through their stories and their lives, we see how leadership in creative fields can be a transformative force.

This lesson will break down their leadership strategies and offer practical advice on how you can apply these lessons to your own creative endeavors. By studying their journeys, you'll gain insights into how leadership can enhance your ability to guide teams, collaborate effectively, and push your creative projects forward.

Alongside these stories, I'll share case studies from my own experiences, where leadership made a difference in global projects. For instance, Stinson Brand Innovation was built on leadership principles that emphasize collaboration, open communication, and a creative workspace where all ideas are valued. And, a merger with GSW Worldwide challenged me to adapt to a larger organization, teaching me the importance of influence, networking, and navigating complex team dynamics without formal authority. In both cases, my leadership style fostered a culture of empowerment and innovation. These reflections provide actionable insights into the importance of leadership in navigating challenges and ensuring the success of creative ventures.

The goal of this lesson is to help you step confidently into leadership roles within your creative work, using the lessons learned from those who have paved the way. By embracing leadership, you'll not only advance your own career but also contribute to the success of those around you, strengthening the entire creative community.

Creative leadership is about empowering others, embracing collaboration, and driving creative efforts toward shared success. Whether you're leading a team or guiding your own career, becoming a creative leader requires embracing opportunities for growth, empowering those around you, and leading with a clear vision.

Janet Attwood: 'The Passion Test'

Janet Attwood is a leader in helping creatives and individuals identify their true purpose through "The Passion Test." Her approach emphasizes the importance of authenticity and encourages people to align their lives with their passions.

During our interview, Attwood highlighted how authenticity helps creatives embrace their true selves and focus on what matters most. Her "Passion Test" is designed to guide individuals toward discovering their core passions, helping them make decisions that lead to a life of meaning and fulfillment.

Attwood applies her principles across different areas, including business, children, and teens, emphasizing that clarity in one's passion influences all aspects of life. She teaches that by identifying what matters most, people can more easily move toward their goals, whether in health, career, or personal relationships.

Her approach includes techniques like "The Work" by Byron Katie and "Mor Up," both of which focus on removing limiting beliefs and fostering gratitude. By encouraging a mindset shift, Attwood helps creatives break free from the barriers that often block their creative flow.

Attwood also shares her own creative routine, which includes practices like meditation, self-reflection, and gratitude. These practices allow her to stay connected to her creativity and maintain resilience in the face of challenges.

In essence, Janet Attwood offers tools and strategies that empower individuals to live purpose-driven lives. Through her work with "The Passion Test" and her focus on removing mental blocks, she encourages people to embrace their creativity and lead with authenticity.

Dr. Bill Dorfman: Dentist to the Stars

Dr. Bill Dorfman has built a career that blends dentistry, entrepreneurship, and philanthropy in ways that have significantly influenced the field of cosmetic dentistry and beyond. Known as the "dentist to the stars," Dr. Dorfman's creativity and business acumen helped him rise to prominence, not just as a clinician but as a leader in his industry.

Dr. Dorfman understood early in his career that a smile is more than just an aesthetic feature. He saw firsthand the psychological transformation that a confident smile can bring to people's lives, helping them overcome insecurities and make stronger personal connections. His approach to dentistry was always about more than fixing teeth; it was about transforming lives through confidence-building.

A key aspect of Dr. Dorfman's leadership is his dedication to mentorship. Through the LEAP Foundation, he teaches young people essential skills like communication and networking, aiming to equip the next generation with the tools to succeed. LEAP is a reflection of Dr. Dorfman's belief that true leadership is about giving back and helping others reach their potential.

One of his most significant achievements was the creation of Discus Dental, where he combined his creative instincts with sharp business strategy. By observing the best practices of Beverly Hills' top dentists and applying them to his own brand, he was able to build a dental practice that stood out in the crowded market. His decision to bring in a publicist was pivotal, propelling his brand to greater visibility and success.

Dr. Dorfman's public breakthrough came with his role on *Extreme Makeover*, which gave him the opportunity to merge his clinical work with media exposure. Through the show, he successfully introduced his Zoom teeth-whitening product to a broader audience, driving its sales and expanding his business. His ability to use media as a strategic tool highlights the importance of creativity in branding, showing how innovation can turn a product into a household name.

Despite his many achievements, Dr. Dorfman stresses the importance of resilience and continuous learning. He believes that staying at the forefront of industry advancements and embracing new technology is essential for long-term success. His story serves as a reminder to creatives and professionals alike that ongoing growth is a key part of leadership.

Beyond his professional achievements, Dr. Dorfman's philanthropy plays a significant role in his life. His philosophy, "learn, earn, and return," drives his commitment to giving back, particularly through his work with the LEAP Foundation. He sees success not just as a personal milestone but as an opportunity to uplift others and make a positive impact on the community.

In conclusion, Dr. Bill Dorfman exemplifies a leader who has successfully integrated creativity, entrepreneurship, and service. His journey shows how using creative strategies, staying focused on personal development, and giving back to others can lead to profound success, both personally and professionally.

Jonathan Knight:
Head of Games, *New York Times*

Jonathan Knight, Head of Games at the *New York Times*, brings over two decades of experience from the world of digital gaming to an organization traditionally known for its journalism. With a career at companies like WB Games, Zynga, and Electronic Arts, Knight's move to NYT Games showcases how media consumption is evolving to include entertainment and interactive experiences alongside news.

Knight explains that the NYT Games division centers on digital puzzles, such as the famous *New York Times* crossword, as well as newer creations like Spelling Bee and Wordle. His leadership has been instrumental in translating these traditional puzzles into digital formats, making them more accessible to a broader audience. The acquisition of Wordle, in particular, was a strategic move designed to attract younger users and funnel them into the NYT's more established offerings like the crossword.

The role of games at the NYT is twofold: they provide entertainment and subscriber retention. Knight emphasizes that games keep readers engaged on a daily basis, which helps counter the more sporadic nature of news consumption. The habit-forming nature of puzzles creates a consistent interaction with subscribers, enhancing loyalty and engagement over time. Although some may see games as a distraction from the news, Knight views them as an essential component of the NYT's growth strategy, playing a key role in maintaining subscriber interest.

Creatively, Knight highlights the trial-and-error process that goes into game development. While innovation is key, he stresses the importance of maintaining the quality of legacy products like the crossword. His leadership encourages a balance between creative experimentation and quality control, ensuring that new projects like Wordle don't overshadow the core puzzles that have made the NYT Games division a success.

In terms of team dynamics, Knight has successfully led teams in a remote and hybrid environment. He emphasizes the importance of having a shared vision and clear communication, ensuring that all team members stay aligned on goals. This is particularly vital in creative fields like gaming, where collaboration is key to producing high-quality products.

Beyond his role at NYT Games, Knight is committed to fostering creativity and innovation in education. He actively volunteers with the Gwinnett County school system in Georgia, where he judges student video game contests. His dedication to mentoring young people in the field of game development demonstrates his belief in the importance of nurturing future creative leaders.

For aspiring creatives, Knight offers clear advice: learn by doing, maintain a growth mindset, and view failure as a learning opportunity. He encourages creatives to surround themselves with supportive teams that promote learning from mistakes and continuously strive for improvement. His leadership at the intersection of media and gaming showcases how adaptability, innovation, and collaboration are essential traits in today's dynamic creative industries.

YaYa Zazueta: Alma de Pueblo

Oralia Zazueta, known by everyone as "YaYa", is the driving force behind Alma de Pueblo, a brand inspired by the traditions of Ures, Sonora, Mexico. YaYa's vision goes beyond simply marketing local foods and products. Through Alma de Pueblo, she aims to celebrate the heritage of her community while ensuring that the skills and traditions that have been passed down through generations are preserved for the future.

Alma de Pueblo features eight carefully curated products, including 100% roasted Mexican coffee, traditional Spanish jamoncillos (sweet candies), and regional delicacies like pipitorias, machaca, and obleas. These items are packaged in beautifully designed gift boxes, providing customers with a way to experience the flavors and craftsmanship of Ures all at once. YaYa's approach is rooted in authenticity, offering a genuine taste of the town's culinary and cultural traditions.

But Alma de Pueblo is not just about selling products—it's a social enterprise with a larger mission. YaYa is deeply committed to addressing the educational needs of the local community and raising awareness about the social issues faced by the people of Ures. By creating a platform for these local products, she is not only generating income for the community but also ensuring that the skills and traditions behind these items are passed on to future generations.

YaYa's leadership is evident in her efforts to build connections between Ures and the wider world, using Alma de Pueblo to tell the story of her community. She works tirelessly to ensure that the cultural identity of Ures is preserved, even as the world around it changes. Her brand is a beacon of tradition, supporting local artisans and farmers while fostering pride in the region's unique heritage.

As a community leader, YaYa plays a vital role in advocating for the needs of Ures. Her dedication to uplifting the community through education, awareness, and economic opportunity has made her a trusted and respected figure. Through Alma de Pueblo, she is creating a legacy that honors the past while building a sustainable future for the people of Ures.

*****

As we've seen through the stories of Attwood, Dorfman, Knight, and Zazueta, creative leadership is about more than just guiding others—it's about stepping into a role where you inspire, innovate, and elevate those around you. These individuals embody the essence of creative leadership, using their unique talents and visions to shape not only their own paths but also the communities and industries they touch.

Their journeys remind us that leadership in the creative realm isn't just about having a title or position; it's about taking ownership of your vision, creating opportunities for collaboration, and building something meaningful that can stand the test of time. Whether it's in business, media, or a local community, creative leaders drive progress by harnessing their passion, engaging with others, and turning obstacles into opportunities.

Now, as we shift from their experiences to my own, the focus turns to the practical application of these lessons. The path to creative leadership is open to anyone willing to embrace the challenge— whether it's leading oneself through personal creative growth, guiding a team toward a common vision, or impacting a broader community with innovative thinking.

This lesson, and indeed this entire book, serves as an invitation for you to step into that role. It's a call to lead creatively—to take ownership of your journey, to inspire others by your example, and to push the boundaries of what's possible in your own sphere. In the following sections, I will share my own experiences navigating the challenges of creative leadership, illustrating how the lessons from these stories, coupled with strategic foresight and adaptability, can serve as a roadmap for leading in creative ways, whether on a personal, professional, or community level.

Founding and Growing My Brand Consultancy

In 2004, I founded Stinson Brand Innovation as a solo endeavor, guided by a vision of merging creativity with strategic branding. What began as a one-person consultancy has since grown into a dynamic, collaborative business shaped by principles of creative leadership.

In the early years, I wore many hats—handling strategy, client relations, and project execution myself. Creativity wasn't just a service we offered; it was the way we operated, shaping every project and client interaction. While my entrepreneurial spirit drove the company forward, I soon realized that this journey wasn't one to be taken alone.

One of my earliest lessons was the importance of empowering the team. I wanted Stinson Brand Innovation to be a place where every person's voice mattered and each team member was empowered to contribute their unique skills and ideas. Creativity thrives in environments where collaboration is central, and I made it a priority to cultivate a workplace where formalities were minimized and open communication was encouraged.

As the company expanded, I focused on creating an atmosphere of trust and flexibility. We reduced unnecessary interruptions, kept rules light, and encouraged both work and play. Informal brainstorming sessions became the norm, and I prioritized a comfortable and practical workspace where ideas could flow freely.

Leadership taught me the importance of balancing intuition with analysis. While I often relied on instinct and spontaneity when making decisions, I soon learned that careful consideration and consistency were crucial. As a leader, I needed to ensure that while we pursued creative solutions, we also made decisions rooted in sound judgment and foresight.

Along the way, I encountered challenges that tested my leadership style. One of the hardest lessons was learning to gather more information before making key decisions. In striving to maintain harmony and preserve relationships, I occasionally hesitated to address tough situations directly. Over time, I realized that facing challenges head-on and making informed, timely decisions were essential to both leadership and the company's success.

Today, as I look back, Stinson Brand Innovation is a testament to the power of collaboration, leadership, and creativity. The growth of the company from its humble beginnings as a solo venture to a thriving consultancy is a reflection of our team's dedication to innovation. Our success wasn't just about individual creative ideas—it's about the collective strength of the team working together toward a shared vision.

Stinson Brand Innovation became more than just a business—it's a reflection of the leadership principles we've developed and the creative environment we've fostered.

My Experience in Merging with GSW Worldwide

When I joined GSW Worldwide in Columbus, OH, it marked a major shift in my professional journey. Moving from leading smaller teams to joining an organization with nearly 500 colleagues required a new approach to leadership—one that relied on influence rather than formal authority. Without a clear title or a place in the official hierarchy, I had to adapt quickly to lead effectively in this much larger structure.

Networking, which had been more peripheral in my previous roles, became essential. GSW's expansive network provided opportunities for collaboration on a scale I hadn't previously experienced. Building relationships and tapping into the wealth of knowledge within the company allowed me to make an impact, even without formal leadership status. The challenge was not just maintaining my own productivity but ensuring I aligned with the collective rhythm of such a large team.

At GSW, there were new layers of bureaucracy and procedures, but I made it a priority to focus on active engagement with the team. I learned to minimize the impact of paperwork and red tape by staying involved with projects at a grassroots level. I shifted from handling all planning and preparation on my own to collaborating with colleagues who brought different perspectives and expertise to the table. This new approach enriched our work and made the process more efficient.

Frequent update meetings were essential to keeping projects on track. I learned that effective leadership in this environment demanded precise delegation and ensuring every team member clearly understood their role. The fast-paced nature of GSW required me to adjust to more regular interactions with management, seeking guidance and support more often than I had in previous roles.

One of the most important lessons I learned was the need for freedom from excessive controls. GSW encouraged independence and agility, which aligned well with my leadership philosophy. I worked hard to create a space where the team could operate creatively and flexibly, free from unnecessary oversight. At the same time, I recognized the importance of understanding the culture and systems in place at GSW. Missteps in such a large organization could have far-reaching consequences, so being mindful of the existing structures was key.

In the end, my transition to GSW Worldwide required a complete evolution of my leadership style. No longer leading from the front in a traditional sense, I learned to lead by facilitating connections, fostering collaboration, and empowering others to take charge. It was a transformative experience that expanded my understanding of what it means to be a creative leader in a fast-paced, complex organization. Through collaboration and adaptability, I was able to navigate the intricacies of this new environment and emerge with a broader, more dynamic approach to leadership.

A Final Word

This lesson has explored creative leadership, drawing inspiration from notable leaders like Janet Attwood, Dr. Bill Dorfman, Jonathan Knight, and YaYa Zazueta. Their stories illustrate the transformative power of leadership in creative fields, offering concrete lessons on how visionaries can inspire change and innovation in their industries. The lesson serves as an invitation for creatives to step into leadership roles with intention, guided by practical wisdom.

The insights in this chapter are not abstract ideas but actionable strategies that can help creatives develop their leadership styles and lead more effectively. These stories, coupled with case studies from my own journey, highlight the importance of leadership in navigating challenges, driving innovation, and fostering growth. Through these narratives, readers can see how leadership principles like collaboration, vision, and adaptability are key to long-term success.

- Janet Attwood emphasizes living with purpose and unlocking creativity through "The Passion Test." Her approach helps creatives overcome self-limiting beliefs and align their lives with their passions.

- Dr. Bill Dorfman, a leading cosmetic dentist, combines his creativity with business acumen. His work with the LEAP Foundation illustrates his dedication to mentoring young leaders and fostering a positive impact.

- Jonathan Knight, Head of NYT Games, demonstrates how creativity and business can work hand in hand, showing how games contribute to the *New York Times'* subscriber retention strategy and growth.

- Oralia (YaYa) Zazueta, through Alma de Pueblo, shows the importance of creative leadership in preserving cultural traditions and promoting social causes in her community in Ures, Mexico.

- At Stinson Brand Innovation, my leadership focused on fostering an open and collaborative environment, empowering team members to contribute their ideas and work toward common goals.

- My experience merging with GSW Worldwide presented new challenges in leadership, teaching me to adapt and lead through influence rather than authority, while navigating the complexities of a larger organization.

Leadership is not about hierarchy but about empowering others, fostering collaboration, and steering creative efforts toward collective success. Whether you're guiding a team or navigating your own creative journey, embracing leadership can unlock new levels of achievement—not just for yourself, but for those around you. A clear vision and a well-defined roadmap can help cultivate the leader within every creative individual, providing the direction and confidence needed to push boundaries and spark innovation. True leadership lies in inspiring growth, championing new ideas, and fostering an environment where success is shared. By stepping into this role with intention and purpose, you contribute to a thriving creative community where collaboration fuels progress and bold ideas shape the future.

Key Takeaways

- Whether you're leading a team or simply charting your own path, embracing your role as a creative leader can unlock new levels of success, not only for yourself but for those around you.

- A roadmap can nurture the leader within every creative individual.

- Leadership means inspiring growth, innovation, and shared success within the broader creative community.

Questions

1. How can Janet Attwood's emphasis on authenticity and self-connection serve as a model for your own leadership style, both personally and professionally?

2. In what ways can you apply "The Passion Test" to identify and align with your deepest passions, fostering a clearer vision for your life in various aspects such as career, relationships, and personal well-being?

3. How does Dr. Bill Dorfman's integration of creativity in cosmetic dentistry and his commitment to philanthropy

inspire you to leverage your creative instincts for both professional success and societal impact?

4. Considering Jonathan Knight's unconventional journey from traditional gaming companies to the New York Times, how can you embrace unexpected opportunities in your career and adapt to the evolving landscape of your industry?

5. Reflecting on Knight's approach to game development, how can you balance innovation and maintaining core values in your creative projects? Additionally, how might you foster collaboration and shared values within your creative team, especially in a remote or hybrid work environment?

6. Reflect on YaYa Zazueta's leadership as a community leader for Alma de Pueblo. How does her approach to empowering the community and sustaining traditions resonate? In what ways can you integrate empowerment into your leadership style?

7. Consider my transition from a solo-preneur to a collaborative leader in Stinson Brand Innovation and then adaptation to a new role in the large GSW office. What lessons can be drawn from these experiences regarding the importance of adaptation and flexibility in leadership? How can you apply these lessons to navigate changes in your professional journey?

8. How does environment foster creativity, collaboration, and a sense of community? What elements from this vision can you incorporate into your own work environment or leadership approach to enhance creativity and team cohesion?

CONCLUSION

Finding your creative spark can feel like looking for a needle in a haystack. We all want to create something that resonates, something that shows who we are. But how do we get there? What makes certain creatives truly stand out?

To find the answers, I spent several months talking with 250 talented people from all sorts of creative fields. Their stories and insights led to some powerful lessons—practical steps you can use to unlock your own creativity and light up your artistic journey. Whether you're already creating and looking for fresh inspiration, or just starting out, the ideas shared here are meant to guide and encourage you in pursuing what you're passionate about.

As we wrap up, I'm reminded of a childhood memory I shared at the start: my second-grade art show in my garage, where friends' artwork lined the walls. That small event shaped how I saw creativity and eventually inspired me to learn from creatives worldwide. Now, I hope these lessons will spark new ideas for you, too, as you step into your own creative world.

1. Identifying Your Signature Methods

Creativity is not a nebulous force; it's a skill that can be honed and refined. Our exploration into the power of signature methods underscored the importance of developing a unique approach to creativity. We learned that creating a distinctive method not only fuels our creativity but also leaves an indelible mark on our endeavors.

Takeaway: Develop Your Signature Method. Discover what makes your creative process unique and leverage it to amplify your impact.

2. Building a Backbone of Resilience

Resilience emerged as the unyielding backbone of every creative journey. Through stories of setbacks, challenges, and triumphs, we witnessed how great creatives bounce back from adversity. Embracing failure all echoes the sentiment that resilience is not just about endurance but about turning challenges into stepping stones for growth.

Takeaway: Embrace Resilience. See challenges as opportunities, and cultivate resilience as an enduring companion on your creative path.

3. Partnering with Collaborators

Creativity finds its zenith in collaboration. The tales of partnerships and collaborations among our guests, illuminating the profound impact of working together. True innovation often emerges at the intersection of diverse perspectives, emphasizing that creativity thrives in a collaborative ecosystem.

Takeaway: Cultivate Collaborative Spirit. Actively seek and embrace collaborations that enhance the richness and depth of your creative endeavors.

4. Mastering the Numbers of Your Business

For creatives, mastering the business side of creativity is as vital as the creative process itself. My guests' strategic approach to branding and marketing demonstrated the importance of understanding the numbers behind creativity. Whether it's managing a creative project budget or navigating the dynamic landscape of media consumption, a creative mind armed with business acumen is a formidable force.

Takeaway: Blend Artistry with Business. Equip yourself with the skills to navigate the business aspects of your creativity, ensuring sustainability and success.

5. Anticipating Obstacles in Your Creative Process

The path to creativity is riddled with obstacles, but adept creatives navigate them with foresight and preparation. Examining stories of overcoming obstacles emphasized the importance of having a contingency plan. A creative journey is not linear, but those who prepare for detours often find unexpected gems along the way.

Takeaway: Plan for the Unexpected. Anticipate obstacles, and craft contingency plans that allow you to adapt and thrive in the face of challenges.

6. Developing Your Leadership Influence as a Creative Force

Leadership in the realm of creativity is not just about guiding others; it's about inspiring and embodying the creative spirit. Janet Attwood's holistic mentorship, Dr. Bill Dorfman's commitment to philanthropy, and Jonathan Knight's dedication to fostering creativity in education all point to the transformative power of creative leadership. It's evident that the mark of a true creative leader is leaving a legacy that extends beyond personal success.

Takeaway: Lead with Purpose. Whether in your creative projects or in guiding others, lead with authenticity, purpose, and a commitment to positive impact.

Living on Purpose and Constant Growth

Purpose is the heartbeat of creativity. Whether in your projects or guiding others, the sixth lesson urged creatives to lead with authenticity, purpose, and a commitment to positive impact. Your creative pursuits gain profound meaning when aligned with a purpose beyond personal satisfaction. Purpose-driven leadership not only inspires but leaves a lasting imprint on the creative landscape.

In tandem with these collective insights, I turned the lens inward, reflecting on my own strengths, weaknesses, successes, and failures. Living on purpose emerged as a recurring theme, emphasizing the importance of having a sense of purpose and worthy goals to build a strong foundation for a successful life.

A Word about Living with *Intention*:

As a naturally intuitive individual, I resonate with the recognition of unusual opportunities during the planning process. Independence and a desire for control are familiar traits, yet the value of diverse viewpoints is acknowledged. The tendency to accept additional work without careful consideration strikes a chord, emphasizing the need to delegate and provide others with valuable experiences.

My world, rich with possibilities and different ways of doing things, mirrors the challenge of concentration on a single task without succumbing to the allure of another. Seeking balance in personal and professional life becomes a conscious effort, requiring care to maintain. While simplicity appeals, the desire for quick answers prompts a reminder to not overlook essential details.

The pursuit of new projects and ideas, relevant or not to the current role, resonates with a thirst for ongoing learning and a drive for new experiences. In the quest for ambitions, active involvement of others is a principle embraced, acknowledging the collective strength in shared endeavors.

Challenges, though seemingly undaunting, may prompt a need for more thorough preparation. The involvement of prestigious individuals in the pursuit of ambitions aligns with a recognition of the value of influential connections.

Let's keep connecting, listening, and learning.

As I wrap up this journey, the lessons I've learned from creative voices around the world are more than just insights—they're a reminder of how we grow, both in our craft and in ourselves. Through these shared stories and personal reflections, creativity becomes more than just a process; it's a part of our everyday lives, unfolding in new ways as we go.

Thank you for joining me in exploring creativity from every angle. I hope these insights inspire you to keep pushing forward, to find resilience in the process, and to bring your unique ideas to life.

So, go out there and create freely. Your imagination has no limits—make it yours, and let it show you what's possible.

Then, you'll unlock your own world of creativity.

ACKNOWLEDGMENTS

This book would not be possible without the voices, experiences, and generous insights of the more than 250 creatives I interviewed from around the world. Your stories have not only enriched these pages but also inspired countless others to unlock their own creative potential.

A heartfelt thank you to my collaborators and supporters who made this project a reality. The initial concept and early interviews with G. Mark Phillips laid the groundwork for what would become a global exploration of the creative spirit. I especially thank Michelle Wangari for her invaluable support in scheduling interviews, transcribing conversations, and summarizing key highlights. Her attention to detail and commitment to this project helped shape so many podcast episodes. Special thanks to podcasting business experts who shared their knowledge and helped elevate the quality of the show: Josh Cary, Luis Ryan Diaz, and Eric Cabral. Your lessons on storytelling, production, and strategy had a profound impact on how the podcast grew and connected with listeners.

I'm deeply grateful to Dr. Christopher Driscoll, who served as my developmental editor, helping structure the stories and frame the reader journey with clarity and purpose.

Special acknowledgment to Insights Learning and Development Ltd. for the use of concepts drawn from my DISC profile. Their framework is copyrighted by Andrew Lothian, Insights, Dundee,

Scotland. It provided meaningful reference points for understanding my own creative energy and leadership.

To the clients I've worked with across the years—you've trusted me to bring creativity into your brands, your strategies, and your breakthroughs. Your belief in my ideas (and your occasional redirection to focus them) has truly meant the world.

Thank you for joining me in this exploration of creativity. Here's to unlocking your own world of possibility.

ABOUT THE AUTHOR

Mark Stinson is a brand innovator and host of the podcast, YOUR WORLD OF CREATIVITY.

In Mark's extensive career, he has dedicated himself to pursuing strategy — for individuals, teams, and organizations. Through his books, publications, talks, and workshops, Mark empowers others with their unique tools to succeed. His podcast serves as a portal into the creative process. From publishing, film, animation, music, restaurants, and medical research, each episode explores creativity across diverse fields.

Mark is a frequent speaker, trainer, and facilitator for sales meetings, advisory boards, and strategy workshops. He is the author of business books, including *Patient Activation, ForwardFast Branding, Customer CHEMistry*, and *N-of-8 Creative Groups*. He has contributed to two motivational books, *Living in the Now* and *Alone In My Universe*.

In addition, Mark is a partner in a local coffee shop, Eagle Coffee & Bakery, where he is creating a community café experience for friends, families, and coworkers.

OTHER BOOKS BY THE AUTHOR

ForwardFast Branding: The 6 Step Model to Accelerate Your Health, Science, and Tech Accelerate complex health and tech brands from concept to clinic with Mark Stinson's proven six step innovation roadmap.

N of 8: A Creative Group Innovation Model for Health, Science, & Technology Brands Unlock razor sharp customer insights with the definitive guide to designing and leveraging high impact eight person focus groups.

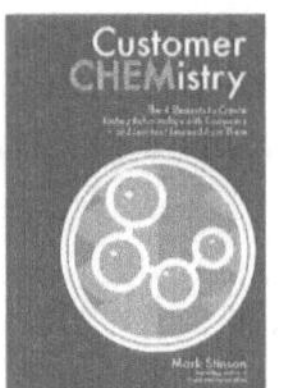

Customer CHEMistry: The 4 Elements to Create Lasting Customer Relationships Fuse communication, honesty, ease, and motivation into an irresistible formula that turns casual buyers into lifelong brand advocates.

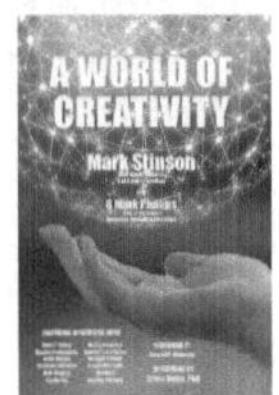

A World of Creativity Travel the globe through inspiring interviews and steal the practical tactics today's innovators use to reignite everyday creativity.

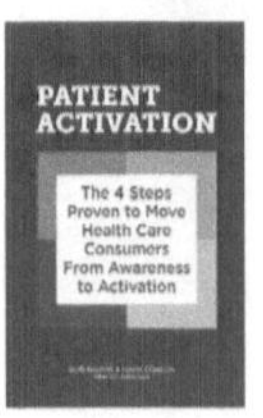

Patient Activation: 4 Steps Proven to Move Health Care Consumers from Awareness to Activation This four-point system empowers patients and supercharges results across any health care initiative.

PODCASTS BY THE AUTHOR

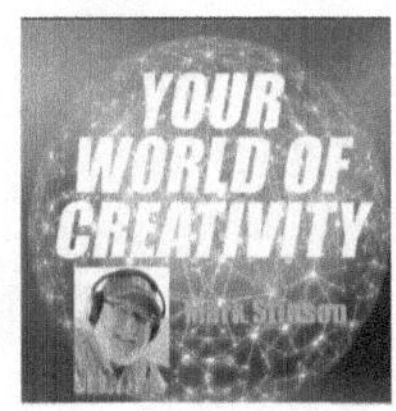

Unlocking Your World of Creativity
Plug into candid conversations with world class creators—learn their tools, spark fresh ideas, and launch your own work into the spotlight.

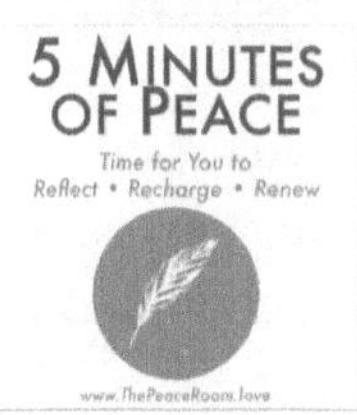

5 Minutes of Peace
Tap play anytime for a five minute reset of mindful meditations and uplifting wisdom from The Peace Room.

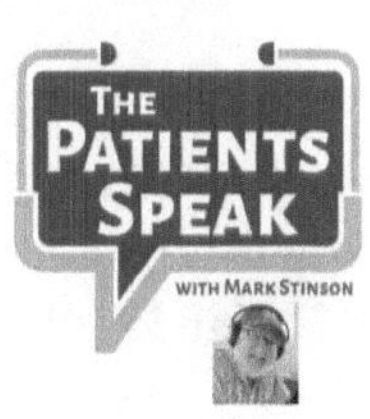

The Patients Speak
Where breakthrough healthcare meets real world voices—hear patient insights and the innovators transforming every step of the journey.

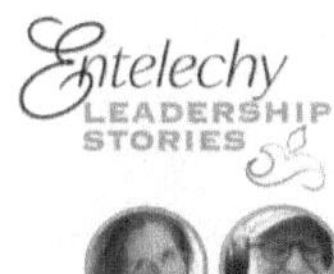

Entelechy Leadership Stories
Discover how conscious leaders turn vision and values into high impact organizations—and learn to unlock your own leadership potential.

Discover More with Exact Rush

If you've enjoyed *UNLOCK Your World of Creativity* by Mark Stinson, we invite you to explore other titles from Exact Rush Multimedia Publishing.

Explore Our Catalog

At Exact Rush, we pride ourselves on a rich selection of titles that focus on creative transformation, spiritual empowerment, and identity. From insightful, cerebral non-fiction, to imaginative works that transports you to different realms or teach you something new, our catalog of accurate, informative, and life-affirming titles continues to grow.

Connect with Our Community

Join our community of readers and authors! Participate in engaging discussions, author meet-and-greets, and exclusive book events. Stay updated by following us on social media and subscribing to our newsletter.

Have a Book Idea?

Do you have a story to tell or knowledge to share? Exact Rush is always on the lookout for unique voices and compelling content. If you have a book idea that aligns with our ethos, we would love to hear from you. Our team is dedicated to nurturing and promoting new talent.

Contact Us

To explore our catalog, learn more about our events, or discuss a book idea, please visit exactrush.com or contact us at exactrushllc@gmail.com. Your journey with Exact Rush doesn't end here. Let's continue to explore, learn, and grow together.